Détente and Socialist Democracy

Détente and Socialist Democracy

A Discussion with Roy Medvedev

Essays from East and West by
Yvan Craipeau, Tamara Deutscher, Ernest Mandel,
Franz Marek, Mihailo Markovic, Ralph Miliband,
George Novack, Michel Pablo, Roger Pannequin,
Jiri Pelikan and E. P. Thompson

on a theme proposed and developed by
Roy Medvedev

Edited for the Bertrand Russell Peace Foundation by
Ken Coates

European Socialist Thought Series No. 6
Spokesman Books
1975

Published by the Bertrand Russell Peace Foundation Ltd
Bertrand Russell House
Gamble Street, Nottingham
for *Spokesman Books*

Printed in Great Britain by
Goodwin Press Ltd
135 Fonthill Rd, London N4

KEN COATES

A General Introduction to the Series

Having passed through a veritable Dark Age, in which dogmatism and obscurantism held a world-wide predominance, and flourished alongside small-minded provinciality, socialist thought has, during the past two decades, undergone a veritable renaissance, affecting almost every major European country, East or West. The collapse of Stalinist orthodoxy has been accompanied by a renewal of radical thinking in some of the older social-democratic and communist parties, and the growth of several independent schools of young intellectuals who have been profoundly influenced by ideas of socialist humanism.

Unfortunately, much of the most audacious and relevant thinking in France, Italy, Hungary, Yugoslavia, Belgium and Germany has been kept out of reach in Britain by a combination of difficulties: commercial publishers have been conservative in taking on commitments unless the authors in question have been glamorous, publicity-attractive figures; all those works which have had a strong empirical base in the experience of a national labour movement have tended to escape translation because it is widely assumed that the English-speaking public is not interested in the detailed sociology of other European countries; and the specialist socialist publishing houses have been highly selective in their choice of doctrinal filters for a variety of reasons.

Extracts from the writings of such men as Mallet, Markovic or Goldmann have been featured in the periodical press in Britain, and some of the specialist works of these authors have found respectable imprints. But not only have major works escaped translation: so too have numerous practical, polemical and agitational writings, some of which are of very great interest to all socialists.

The object of this series is to begin to remedy some of these deficiencies. It is hoped to make available a number of important original works of analysis as well as some more directly propagandist essays which will assist the Labour Movements of the English-speaking world to understand their colleagues. But it is also hoped that the series may assist in widening the dialogue between socialists in East and West Europe, and emphasizing the organic unity of their interests and concerns.

Contents

Acknowledgements

We are grateful to *New Left Review*, who have generously granted permission to republish Roy Medvedev's first essay in this book, originally featured in their January 1973 number (83). All the contributors to this symposium have given their work without fee, as an act of solidarity both with Roy Medvedev and with the Bertrand Russell Peace Foundation, which is currently suffering acute financial difficulties as a result of official harassment. So have the translators, who have laboured assiduously to produce clear texts in a very short time. They are: Tamara Deutscher, who translated the pieces from Roy Medvedev's Russian originals; Steve Bodington, who provided the English versions of the items by Roger Pannequin and Yvan Craipeau; and Chris Goodey, who translated the article by Michel Pablo.

George Novack's article has previously been published by *Intercontinental Press*, and Michel Pablo's by *Sous le Drapeau du Socialisme*. Ralph Miliband's essay is part of a longer work, entitled *Stalin and After*, which first appeared in *The Socialist Register*, 1975. We are grateful for permission to reprint these pieces.

And we are above all grateful to Roy Medvedev, whose courageous and firmly rational commitment gives us real reason for hope that good sense may ultimately prevail over an irrational international polity whose follies are by no means all rooted in his own part of the world.

Introduction

To those of us who remember, with great unease, the horrors
of McCarthyism in the United States and of the Zdhanovschina
in the Soviet Union, it has always been a lively hope that détente
between the powers would bring greater freedom and more
rational standards of political discourse. For a time it seemed
possible that our hopes would be immediately justified. As the
'thaw' set in, it seemed that a notable liberalization had begun
on both sides of the cold war divide. But this appearance did not
last very long. From the United States, a series of Central Intelligence Agency initiatives, involving armed interventions, assassi-
nations of heads of states, and a plethora of sophisticated dirty
tricks, extended the sway of repressive regimes around the world
and built up the insidious hold of the Watergate machine on
domestic policy in the metropolis itself. In the USSR the fall of
Khrushchev was followed by a partial exhumation of Stalin,
intensified repression, and intensified dissension. The Warsaw
Pact's invasion of Czechoslovakia set back the European clock
by perhaps a decade, certainly already more than half that long.
The brutal overthrow of President Allende by the Chilean Military Junta blocked hopes of peaceful social change in all but the
most advanced capitalist countries, and seriously undermined
them even there. Around the globe, two decades after the
beginning of détente, political prisoners do not diminish in
number, censorship flourishes, repression of all kinds intensifies
with heightened social conflict. Yet détente remains more than
necessary: it is inevitable, if mankind is to survive.

At this point, I first wrote 'if humanity is to survive'. Are the
two concepts, however, coterminous? Is it possible that mankind
may continue without freedom, without potential, as a licensed
half-species, limited always by the brutal exigencies of counter-

vailing military pressures? Perhaps it is possible, but there are a number of hopeful indicators which show that it is by no means *necessary*.

In the West, these straws in the wind include, in almost every advanced nation, the growth of an informed and radical public opinion which questions, and at times strenuously opposes, the presumed rights of capital to dictate social policy, to determine with whom peace shall flourish and against whom war and repression shall be unleashed, and to form the choices open to people, as to which life-styles shall be adopted, which rejected. This minority opinion has already given rise to a dynamic socialist culture, largely independent of the traditional organizations of the Left, and quite uncontainable within the mold of old dogma. A whole plethora of new journals and newspapers have been created, in which an extraordinary range of views and analyses can be developed. The library which would house the work of these independent socialist thinkers would already need a substantial building and considerable endowments. Not all of the works it might contain would avoid harmful misjudgements. Some would not help the cause of détente, and not all their authors understand why democracy must prosper as a necessary precondition in any beneficial social change: but all do contribute to the generation of a fine critical sense, as the orthodox notions inherited from previous generations of social critics are successively put to scrutiny, challenged, and rejected or refined. As happens in every widely-based progressive movement, some intellectual excesses occur: various forms of nonsense achieve a temporary vogue, and various half-truths come to serve as the bases for ill-constructed theoretical models. Even so, there have already been times when these rebellious currents of thought have exercised significant influence on a world scale: notably in the early days of opposition to the American intervention in Vietnam, when their initiative in Europe and the United States itself produced a huge popular movement with an élan and imaginative capacity far outside the range of the much larger traditional organizations of the labour and socialist movements. It is earnestly to be hoped that a similar movement can be created in time to prevent foreign intervention in Portugal, and to allow the Portuguese people the scope to develop their own democratic institutions, and their own forms of socialist organization.

The inestimable virtue of this school of young activists is that it offers a real challenge to all the predatory assumptions which have governed the conduct of Western capitalism throughout the postwar decades.

In Eastern Europe and the USSR, this movement is matched by a similar ferment, even if censorship and political discrimination by the authorities are much more intensive, and far more intolerant of independent thought. The lethal weight of repression is still felt in some areas: but between the cracks in the old monolith sprout numberless green shoots, each itself a token of further disintegration of the once-hard stone. Of course, arbitrary rule has given rise to a whole variety of forms of rejection. Some of these take the shape of religious revivals, or nationalist and separatist organizations. Others combine a variety of illusions about the realities of life in the West with some all-too-accurate perceptions about how things are at home, to produce rather anachronistic utopias. Still others re-explore the insights as well as the failings of the old orthodoxy in order to seek for pointers to a more humane society. It is that last group which helps true détente, by reaching towards the transcendence of all those social forms which are most retrogressive in their own lives, and most forbidding to the majority of working people and an important minority of the intelligentsia (that part with open minds) in the West. If John Foster Dulles had never had a Stalin, he would have needed to invent one. Alas, even his powers of invention would have been stretched to the limit before he could have come up with anything half as effective in inhibiting the progress of socialism as the genuine article. So when there emerges a school of socialists, living in the 'socialist' countries, which begins to explore the meaning of socialist democracy, and the ideals of communist humanism, in the light of a truthful appreciation of the social realities bequeathed by Stalin's awful regime, this itself becomes a powerful influence on the socialist movement in the West.

Already this school has been responsible for notable achievements. In Hungary, Andras Hegedus and his colleagues have digested the lessons of the trauma which led up to the 1956 uprising, and began to advance a bold programme not only for democratization, but for the socialization of socialism. Agnes Heller has produced a beautiful little book analysing the concept of need in Marx, which shows in the most contemporary terms how only the widest and most comprehensive democracy can deal with the problems which are left on Marx's agenda. What she says has as much relevance for the growing environmentalist lobby in the West as it has for the development of democratic communism in her own country. Creativity, of course, bears its own penalties, and in Hungary these include exclusion from the Party, from the University, and from the right to foreign travel. No Hungarian could contribute to this present book, because the laws of copyright in Hungary have been cleverly designed to render the unofficial export of a manuscript a criminal offence, as a breach of the exchange control legislation. That manuscripts could imaginably be exported without money changing hands is, apparently, not conceivable in a socialist country. Thus we approach the state in which Man was once supposed to be able to 'hunt in the morning, fish in the afternoon, and critically criticise in the evening'. Hunting and fishing are all right, but critically criticising is, it is to be feared, now considered a diversion of the old bourgeoisie, reserved to ancient malcontents like Karl Marx, and quite, quite unmarxist.

In Yugoslavia, the *Praxis* group of philosophers, whose spokesmen are distinguished humanists like Markovic and Stojanovic, have put forward an extensive critique of current 'socialist' practice. Markovic has shown, in a lucid essay, how the notion of separation of powers has heightened rather than diminished relevance in a society transitional to socialism: and he has advanced a whole series of specific proposals about how the doctrine could be applied in post-capitalist conditions. As a result, in this most liberal of communist countries, the Faculty of Philosophy at Belgrade University has been arbitrarily disbanded, and *Praxis* itself has been suppressed.

In the German Democratic Republic, in Poland, the same

ferment develops, with broadly similar results. In Czechoslovakia, after the military restoration of Winter, thousands of communist academics and professional workers have been downgraded to menial work while cultural life is dominated by timeservers of the crassest stamp.

Alexander Dubcek is relegated to the forestry commission and threatened with arbitrary deportation, and dozens of dedicated socialists, of diverse schools of thought, remain in prison. Even so, the journal *Listy* survives in emigration, and is constantly able to fill its pages with clandestine communications smuggled out from beneath the vigilant gaze of Mr. Husak's not inconsiderable police force.

And in the Soviet Union, among all the legion of critics of every stamp, and all the banned organizations, and in spite of all the hostile pressures, there are the voices of Roy Medvedev and his colleagues. Unlike his better-publicised contemporaries, who often pander to Western vanity by assuming that evil is a Soviet invention, and that repression has been patented for exclusive use in Moscow, Roy Medvedev lives in a world which we can recognize. By careful attention to the facts, strict accuracy in reporting, balanced and rational argument, he holds up, not only before Soviet society, an image of what socialist democracy might be.

If his view prevails, when his view prevails, the détente will be secure: the people of Birmingham, Chicago, Frankfurt and Lyons will see to that. Once the political institutions of the USSR even begin to look as if they can really allow socialist democracy to grow, the last of all the arguments of the western cold warriors will have disappeared. Their interests may remain intransigently greedy and inhuman as always: but they will stand openly exposed, without any of the protective cover which has always up to now shielded them from public understanding. No-one wishes to bomb Leningrad in order to keep America safe for General Motors, except a handful of General Motors' beneficiaries. But millions of Americans will acquiesce in the stockpiling of bombs for Moscow in order to 'defend democracy'. They will see no continuing need, however, to defend democracy against itself. Communist democracy, far from evidencing weakness, will be the most powerful force on earth. Worldwide, it will heal the old breaches in the Labour Movement, isolate the elite groups of financiers and capitalists into a visibly reactionary and obviously anti-democratic clique, and rekindle the hopes of all those who ever dared to nourish hope in a time in which despair has been given a domestic and even comfortable aspect, with all the semblance of permanence, for large populations.

It may be some time before this happens. Until it does, the most important, indeed the only irreversible détente is the one which opens up in the dialogue of the critics, East and West. On what they build, all else will flourish.

It was for this reason that the Bertrand Russell Peace Foundation decided to commission the essays which are published in this book, and to invite Roy Medvedev to consider them, and if possible, reply to them. We were encouraged to do so by Medvedev's own invitation, issued to the world at large in November 1973 in the first Essay which is featured in this volume. Of the many socialists and radicals who were asked to contribute their views on Roy Medvedev's original article, the contributions in this book have been selected as representing a partial cross-section of the widely divergent trends of thought whose spokesmen responded. We do not regard the contributions published here as the end of the argument: rather, we hope this book will be the first of many similar ones, and that soon whole journals and even newspapers will emerge to enable this discussion to develop freely, pursuing the truth wherever it may lead.

A Letter

Dear Ken Coates,

I have received (though with some delay) a great part of the essays on democratization, which will be included in the volume in preparation by the Bertrand Russell Foundation. It was extremely useful for me to read all these essays and I made them known also to many of my friends and other like-minded people.

As I can see, many of the authors of these essays support the main ideas which I expressed in my articles on democratization in 1973-74. But apart from these, the collection also contains various new conceptions as well as critical remarks concerning my views. Many of these critical remarks are undoubtedly justified and I shall certainly take them into consideration in my work. Some, however, have their source in the lack of full understanding of conditions in which we here, in the USSR, have to act.

Unfortunately, the socialist-minded dissidents here represent an intellectual trend only; there is no question, and for the time being there cannot be any question, of any kind of organization or even of any theoretical seminars or debates. And that is why it is simply impossible for us even to pose the problem of 'activity among the working class' for the lack of which some of my critics reproach me.

But for all the disagreements and differences, especially important for me was the spirit of solidarity and support which permeated all the essays without exception, and also the tolerance towards our obvious mistakes and shortcomings, which often stem from our lack of information and from the fact that we have been cut off from the general development of socialist thought.

Recently I have written another essay which also touches upon the questions that constituted the main theses of articles of 1973-74. This essay may perhaps also be useful for the volume which you are now preparing.   With fraternal greetings,

Roy Medvedev

Problems of Democratization and Détente

Some four to five years ago the international situation was still a source of serious anxiety to all who cared for peace, democracy and socialism. The enormous scale of the continuous American intervention in Indochina, the incursion of the Warsaw Pact troops into the territory of the Czechoslovak Socialist Republic, the new Berlin crisis, the armed skirmishes on the Soviet-Chinese border, the acceleration of the arms race all over the world—all these were exacerbating international tensions to the utmost, and encouraging reactionary and extremist forces in every country. Major efforts were needed to change the trend of world events. Today, we know that such efforts were made and that they have achieved quite impressive results. We shall not enumerate here all the agreements and treaties which have critically altered the international atmosphere. It should not be overlooked, however, that the progress of détente over the last three years has been neither smooth nor easy. Initiatives of the USSR have played a very significant role in furthering it. We can assume that the development of the Soviet 'peace offensive' provoked serious disagreements among our leaders.

The main reason for the elimination of Shelest, for example, was certainly not because of his 'nationalist' errors, but because of his objections to Nixon's trip to the USSR in 1972. The pensioning-off of Voronov from the Politbureau was another major setback to rightist circles within our leadership.

International détente was not, of course, the outcome of the Soviet peace offensive alone. It was made possible by mutual concessions, and readiness to compromise on both sides. It is plain that in the Western countries this readiness for compromise likewise emerged only after prolonged and acute political conflicts. The diminution of international tension created conditions not only for limiting *increases* in strategic armaments, but also for *reducing* the military establishments of all the great powers and of many smaller countries, and thereby for accelerating the peaceful economic development of every continent. The improvement of relations between the largest powers on the planet has thus proceeded not at the expense of other countries and nations; it benefits all mankind.

The Current Repression

In the past, the state of armed confrontation between the Great Powers, the 'Cold War' and the debased anti-Soviet and anti-Western propaganda which they exchanged in no way helped to overcome the remnants of Stalinist totalitarianism nor to foster democratic reforms in the USSR. Today, however, we can likewise see that international détente and development of trade and other forms of co-operation, do not automatically lead to changes in the political climate in the Soviet Union, to the growth of democratic freedoms, or to respect for the political and civic rights of the individual, either.

No country in the world has in this century undergone such dramatic and contradictory experiences as the Soviet Union. It was therefore natural that even the insignificant and limited degree of democratization which could be observed in our country between 1961 and 1967, awoke among thinking elements in our society the most diverse political currents, both within the framework of Marxism and without it. Although these trends involved only a minimal fraction of our intelligentsia, this awakening of political thought alarmed the Right within the leadership of the CPSU. This wing of the party is composed of functionaries promoted and formed in the epoch when Soviet society was plunged in utter political passivity and silence, when administrative rather than political methods, coercion rather than persuasion, were used to rule the country.

Various measures to constrict freedom of political discussion within the USSR were introduced by 1967 and at the beginning of 1968. They were notably tightened after August 1968. All political tendencies, 'left' as well as 'right', were attacked, although in differing degree; in recent years, for instance, the most blatant manifestations of Russian chauvinism and open exaltations of Stalin have also been condemned. Subsequent foreign policy successes of the Soviet Union and the slackening of international tension did not put a stop to the assault on 'dissenters'.

In many respects, the pressure against dissent even increased; political trends that had only just started to emerge were stifled and social thought repressed. A considerable number of people, who had much to say, were forced into silence as they were not prepared to put at risk their own apparent freedom or the well-being of their relatives and friends.

This pressure from above in no way excluded recourse to straightforward judicial repressions or even to such inhuman methods of intimidation as shutting sane people up in psychiatric hospitals for patently political reasons. The words and deeds of broken men like Yakir and Krasin were exploited to disintegrate and demoralize oppositionists of past years. Many Western papers long presented Yakir and Krasin as 'courageous fighters for human rights', although the unprincipled and objectively provocative character of their activity had been obvious to a number of people in our country for some years. The strength of various democratic tendencies was also reduced by the noticeable easing of emigration to Israel. Under the influence of the new situation, even those Jews and their relatives who not long before had actively worked for the enlargement of civil rights and liberties in the USSR and had no intention of leaving the country, began to emigrate. Very recently, dispatch abroad of dissenters from other non-Jewish nationalities has also begun, although still experimentally.

For the majority of ordinary 'unorthodox' people or those inclined to be critical of certain aspects of our political and social life, the mounting administrative pressure against all dissent is, however, of the greatest importance. As is well known, in our country the State is not merely the main, it is in fact the only 'employer'. In the absence of all democratic checks or balances, this circumstance affords extremely simple and highly effective means of exerting pressure on people who perform their professional work irreproachably, but are not 'loyal' enough in the opinion of one or another high official. Protests against the restriction of democratic rights in the USSR continues to this day, of course. In some respects they have even intensified and assumed new forms. These protests are, however, more and more made by individuals or, at best by very small groups of people who are protected not so much by democratic traditions or institutions, as by their international reputation and fame. Such people now come forward in a much more active and resolute manner than was possible even for them some years before: they publish their artistic or scientific writings abroad, are interviewed by foreign correspondents, release public statements widely disseminated beyond our frontiers. The activity of these people now arouses a much greater political resonance than ever before, and has become an important element in our political life. Their courage cannot be doubted, and it deserves respect.

Recent Statements by Leading Dissenters

However, it is necessary also to be aware that many of these people live under constant and intense pressure, that they are subjected to crude and unjust abuse in the press and in propaganda by word of mouth, that they are painfully hurt by the persecution and arrests of their less famous colleagues and friends. Deprived of the previous support that has sustained them in a somewhat wider circle of intelligentsia, many of them have begun to express more and more extremist viewpoints, to put forward less and less constructive proposals, being moved more by emotions than by the considerations of political efficacy.

One man, for instance, recently claimed that even blacks in South Africa are not subjected to such cruel persecution and constriction as 'unorthodox thinkers' in the USSR. Another attacked Brandt bitterly and unjustly for his *Ostpolitik*, declaring that Brandt was betraying the interests of democracy in the West and in the East, and that he should be tried by a future Nuremberg Tribunal for war crimes. A third told his friends that Allende's government had led Chile into an impasse from which the only way out was either a 'red' or a 'white' dictatorship, and that in such a situation the military putsch, even with its excesses, was 'the lesser evil' for Chile and its people. A fourth appealed to the American Congress not to encourage trade with the USSR until the Soviet Union conceded full freedom of emigration, as if this were the minimum demand of democracy. Yet it is perfectly obvious that, although the right to leave a country is an important civic freedom, it is much more important to create conditions in the Soviet Union such that its citizens should not desire to leave their own country.

Opinions and statements of this kind, widely publicized in the Western press, are now undoubtedly arousing not only reserve but reprobation among left-wing and democratic circles in the West. At the same time they are also being exploited by reactionary groups in the leadership of our country to increase the pressure on the intelligentsia, and to split and demoralize the ranks of the 'dissenters'.

The clamp-down on the intelligentsia became pronounced at the end of August and the beginning of September 1973, when the Soviet press launched a violent campaign against one of our greatest scientists, the atomic physicist Academician Andrei Sakharov. This assault was also partly directed against the outstanding Russian writer Alexander Solzhenitsyn. What was the background of this campaign? Sakharov and Solzhenitsyn, independently of each other, had given interviews to foreign correspondents in which they expressed their views on many topical questions of international politics and on some concrete internal problems of the Soviet Union. The opinions which the two men expressed were by no means incontrovertible. In itself, therefore, the mere fact that Soviet newspapers published letters from individual readers, or even certain collective communications, criticizing one or other of Sakharov's or Solzhenitsyn's contentions, was not extraordinary. What was objectionable, however, was the fact that in these 'indignant protests' the statements and opinions of Sakharov were largely distorted, while the substance of Solzhenitsyn's declaration was simply suppressed altogether. The overwhelming majority of academicians, writers, workers, employees or technicians who signed these protests, were not acquainted with the full text of the interviews given by either Sakharov or Solzhenitsyn; at best they were shown only some sentences from them taken out of context. We know that many people who did sign the collective declarations were subjected to intense pressures, and that the majority of them had not the slightest idea why Sakharov and Solzhenitsyn gave these interviews to Western correspondents. The main aim of those who organized this vociferous campaign was not to silence Sakharov and Solzhenitsyn; their primary objective was to maximize pressure on other less known 'dissidents' and on the bulk of the thinking intelligentsia. To some extent the campaign obviously achieved this aim, but it had far less success than its initiators had expected.

Explanations of the Clamp-Down

Of course, the aggravation of various forms of harassment of 'dissidents' in the last few months, was not a direct result of the gradual international détente. Yet it does seem that there was a connection between the two processes. It has been suggested, for example, that all the clumsy ideological campaigns of recent months were unleashed by right-wing dogmatic tendencies within the Central Committee of the CPSU independently of the main leadership in the Politbureau, and that the real purpose of these campaigns was to halt the Soviet 'peace offensive' in the international arena, and in particular to disrupt the European Security Conference. This hypothesis rests on the belief that our own 'hawks' sought to provoke a combination of domestic developments and foreign protests against them, of a sort that would inevitably put a stop to any prospect of rapprochement and break up international détente. The result would be to arrest incipient scientific and technical co-operation between the USSR and the West, and to revive the acrimonious polemics with the West, which give the extreme Right of our leadership a particular feeling of well-being.

However, there is another interpretation of the campaign

that is more plausible. Wide-ranging economic co-operation with capitalist countries, abolition of traditional barriers to trade and tourism, limitation and reduction of weapons and armed forces, winding down of the 'Cold War', and in consequence improvement of East-West contacts, naturally demand more mutual confidence at least in international relations. This in turn cannot but affect the field of ideology. A real end to the 'Cold War' and an improvement in the international climate is quite impossible—indeed unthinkable—without the liquidation of all discrimination not only in trade, but also in exchange of information and contact between peoples. The development of international collaboration cannot be achieved without broadening the exchange of men and information: and what is needed to achieve this is, in the first instance, a number of definite concessions on our part—for example, the elimination of such archaic remnants of the Cold War as jamming of foreign radio stations. As is known, the Soviet State broadcasts in all the main languages of the globe, giving its point of view on all world events and also presenting and interpreting developments in our own country. In these circumstances, jamming of Western radio stations which in their transmissions have a different ideological standpoint but a similar functional aim, is discrimination which hinders the process of détente just as much as the possible refusal of the US Congress to grant us the status of 'most favoured nation' in trade.

This concession has already been made: from 21 September 1973 the jamming of the Voice of America, of the BBC, and of the *Deutsche Welle* has ceased. Apparently more facilities will be granted to foreign correspondents in the USSR: they will be able to travel about the country and to make contacts with Soviet citizens. Journalists will have the same rights and facilities as all Soviet correspondents abroad have long had at their disposal. Next on the agenda for settlement will be the question of the reception of American television programmes on Soviet sets and vice versa, transmitted live by satellite; as also that of granting the Soviet people greater opportunities to read Western newspapers, journals, scientific literature, etc. The ratification—long overdue—of UN Charters of social, cultural, economic, political and civic rights is also a positive development.

Obviously, international exchange of ideas and persons calls for a modification of forms and methods of ideological work in the Soviet Union, a greater flexibility in our propaganda and a moratorium on antiquated and dogmatic pronouncements: in other words it calls for a development of Marxism. Under present conditions of ideological struggle, Marxism can only retain influence on the consciousness of people—let alone increase it—by uncompromisingly honest, open and truthful scientific analysis of the totality of contemporary social problems and of the whole unfalsified history of international events and revolutionary experiences of the 20th century.

It is a noticeable fact that the officials and organizations in our country which are in charge of economic questions, foreign affairs and external trade, have proved to be better equipped to work in new conditions than those assigned to ideological problems. Many of the latter have proved incapable of extending the Soviet 'peace offensive' into the ideological arena for which they are responsible. Clearly driven on to the defensive, with no prospects of influencing popular consciousness, our leading ideologues try to cope with new tasks not by adopting new decisions, but by strengthening 'ideological discipline', by intimidating dissenters, by increasing political and moral pressure on Soviet citizens—in other words, not by persuasion but by duress, which in the end is fatal to any ideology.

Factional Struggles within the Party

The contradiction inherent in this situation, and the discrepancies in the handling of external and internal problems (discrepancies which were virtually non-existent in August 1968, but which are very evident today), provide the soil for polemical disputes and factional struggles within the higher echelons of the Central Committee of the CPSU. This type of conflict tends to generate internal mutual accommodation: it is possible that the heightening of pressure on 'dissenters' and the recent laborious campaigns against unorthodoxy were precisely concessions made to the right wing of our leadership in exchange for acceptance of a foreign policy of détente and trade with the West. All this is no more than a hypothesis, of course. The possibility cannot be discounted that no such compromise has occurred, but rather that the entire Politbureau is convinced that only intensification of struggle on the 'ideological front' can fortify this 'front' at home against the prospect of a détente inevitably linked to increased international exchange of men and ideas.

The activity of rightist, reactionary and dogmatic forces in the USSR has not been confined to the 'affair' of Sakharov and Solzhenitsyn; it also left its mark on all the discussions of problems within the social sciences in the first half of 1973. We have been witnessing an obvious deterioration in the field of historical writing, in philosophy, in the debates on many economic problems, as well as in literature and art. This outburst of activity on the Right was undoubtedly occasioned by the détente, which not only seemed dangerous to reactionary forces but actually is dangerous to them, because it weakens their influence in all countries which pass from the phase of confrontation to that of co-operation. In the Soviet Union, however, where moderate and more sober politicians sit in the same Central Committee together with blatant reactionaries and where the struggle is conducted, unseen by society, behind closed doors in the 'corridors of power'—in such conditions the conflict between various groups and tendencies is accompanied by an unmistakable 'cooling' of the whole internal political atmosphere.

How can these regressive tendencies in our internal politics be overcome? In what way can the growing weight of reactionary forces of the Right on cultural and ideological life in the USSR be weakened? The answer to these questions is not easy. There are certainly no quick solutions to the problem. It is clear that the forces of the progressive intelligentsia, including the Party intelligentsia, are still too feeble to oppose the sharp swing to the right in our political and social life. It is also necessary to take into account the political passivity of the working class, of the employees, and even more so of the peasantry. In the apparatus of the Party and the State there are not a few sober people who realize the necessity of changes in domestic politics, but these 'party-democratic' groups have little influence and usually occupy the lower rungs of the official hierarchy.

Change from Above and Change from Below

Any shift towards a more consistent democratization, towards greater tolerance to the 'dissenters', towards a more flexible and reasonable internal policy that would permit the existence of political minorities both inside and outside the framework of Marxism, is at present possible in the USSR only as a result of certain initiatives 'from above' supported 'from below', but not as a sheer result of pressure from 'below'. The need for a thorough-going democratization of Soviet society has long since arrived in the USSR. It is, in fact, the most important precondition for an acceleration of the economic, political, social and cultural development of our country. Only a genuine socialist democracy can give birth to the new motor forces that are necessary to restore health and life to the whole system of Soviet institutions and organizations. The political passivity of our population 'below' is, however, equally obvious. People have learnt to become so silent, and have acquired such a sense of guilt, that no individual dissenters—not even small groups of dissenters—can give rise to a mass movement capable of bringing about any real political change. The masses could move only as a result of serious political or economic crises. Yet the prospect of such crises seems neither probable nor desirable. Soviet society can and will develop even within its existing political structure and economic conditions. Although its development is too slow by the yardstick of the real possibilities of socialism, it is nevertheless sufficient to avert any incontrollable growth of dissatisfaction among broad masses of the people. The economic resources and the natural wealth of the Soviet Union are so great, and the State monopoly of foreign trade safeguards our domestic market so well from undesirable competition, that even under a weak and incompetent leadership, growth in all branches of the national economy will continue.

In such conditions a reorganization of social and economic management, an enlargement of political and civic liberties, an expansion of socialist democracy, can come—as we have said—not as a result of open pressure by the popular masses and the intelligentsia, but as a consequence of initiatives 'from above'. In effect, the exposure of the 'cult of personality' of Stalin at the 20th Congress of the CPSU was in no sense the result of a simple pressure of the masses or the lower ranks of the party. This event, so important for the fate of the whole world communist movement, was the result of some certain struggles 'at the top' whose details have still to be fully clarified, and which reflected a growing dissatisfaction in the country only very obliquely. Likewise, the undeniable 'liberalization', the noticeable loosening of censorship in all fields of intellectual and artistic creativity, as well as many other positive processes which unfolded for some years after the 22nd Congress, were in the first instance the work of the political 'heights'. Of course, the majority of our intelligentsia welcomed the 'thaw', which warmed the atmosphere of our country. However, only a small section of the intelligentsia hastened to avail itself of this 'liberalization', which was why in the sphere of creation of new spiritual values, the results were noticeable, but not very considerable. The majority adopted a waiting attitude, fearing—as it turned out, not without reason—that the 'thaw' might prove temporary and would soon be succeeded by a new period of 'inclemency' in our cultural life.

But if today it is not the outlook of those 'below' that is of decisive importance, but the moods and views of those 'above', how can the political 'heights' be impelled to proceed not towards a further 'tightening of the screws', but towards an enlargement of socialist democracy? It is true, of course, that there exists among the broad masses as well as among the intelligentsia of the USSR a growing frustration and dissatisfaction with many aspects of our society: with the slow tempo of our economic, social, and cultural progress, with our over-centralized and bureaucratized system of management, with waste of resources and lack of information, with failure to catch up with the West in so many respects, and so on. This

mass discontent has an effect in very complicated and round-
about ways on the leadership of the country too. However,
the higher one goes in the ruling hierarchy, the less this pressure of popular dissatisfaction is felt; which is why it cannot
lead to swift changes towards democracy.

The Ambiguity of External Pressures

Thus the idea of increasing pressure from outside tends in-
voluntarily to occur. The impact and influence which international opinion has on the ruling circles of one or another
big or small country should not be underestimated. The general
indignation provoked in the West by the introduction of the
'tax on learning' imposed on emigrants (at present, of course,
the majority of emigrants are Jews), the numerous protests
of public figures and organizations, the debate on the subject
in the US Congress, etc—all these reactions led the Soviet
leadership to drop this tax, although formally it has not been
annulled. Likewise, it was not the remonstrations of Soviet
scientists but the determined protests of Western scientists and
academic institutions against the onset of a shrill campaign
to discredit Academician Sakharov and prepare the ground
for his expulsion from the Academy of Sciences of the USSR
(the demand for which had already appeared in many articles),
that has saved this outstanding Soviet scientist, at least for the
time being, from repression. Again, it was not public opinion
in the USSR, still less our community of writers, but the enormous international prestige of Solzhenitsyn as a Nobel Prize
winner that has restrained the right-wing of the Soviet leadership from settling its accounts with this eminent Russian writer.

At the same time, it is only fair to remark that it was precisely the prolonged pressure not only of American, but also
of international public opinion, that eventually helped to bring
direct American military intervention in Indochina to an end.
Equally, we should not overlook the connection between the recent amnesty granted to political prisoners in Greece and the long
struggle of the progressive forces in Europe for the re-establishment of a democratic regime in Greece. Other examples of the
genuine influence of international public opinion on the course of

political events in one country or another could be adduced; although there is also still a very long list of sombre and tragic occurrences which the public opinion of the West, of the East or even of the whole world, has unfortunately proved only too helpless to avert.

But in one way or another, public opinion constitutes an important force with which any politician today must reckon, including the Soviet leaders. However, it would be a great over-simplification to suppose that it is only with the assistance of pressure from outside, let alone in the field of international relations and trade, that genuine concessions can be gained in the internal politics of a country like the Soviet Union. Pressure from outside can play both a positive and a negative role. It may in some cases restrain our agencies of power from certain deeds, and in other cases it may, on the contrary, provoke them into undesirable action and thereby hinder the democratization of Soviet society.

Thus, for example, it would be unreal to suppose that under pressure from the US Congress the Soviet government would pass a special law allowing everybody who desires to do so to emigrate from the USSR. If the American Congress were to adopt the Jackson Amendment and withdraw the 'most favoured nation' clause in trade relations, this would not improve but harm the prospects of further emigration. Soviet-American relations would also deteriorate. At present work on the draft of a new Constitution for the USSR is in progress. Significant improvements in the sections concerning the civic and political rights of Soviet citizens, and the constitutional guarantees of these rights, are envisaged. The authors of the draft cannot now avoid dealing with such an important democratic freedom as the right to leave one's country and return to it at will. However formal many constitutional rights of Soviet citizens may be, the inclusion in the new Constitution, even with certain reservations, of rights of free entry and exit in the USSR would be extremely important. The adoption by the US Congress of the Jackson Amendment would only lessen the chances of such a clause being included in the new Constitution. For this reason, we consider Academician Sakharov's appeal to Ameri-

can Congressmen to support this amendment to be a mistaken
step, both tactically and substantively.

Appeals to the Western Right

In general, it would be wrong to overestimate the possibility
of achieving results by exercising pressure on the USSR in
the field of diplomatic or economic relations, and not merely
because the Soviet side would reasonably object to interfer-
ence in the internal affairs of the USSR. We very much doubt
that the majority of leading Western statesmen are seriously
concerned with the problems of political and civic rights in
the USSR or in China. In the final analysis, Nixon, Pompidou
and Heath are defending the interests of the ruling classes of
their own countries, and it should by no means be assumed
that capitalist circles in the USA, Britain, France or Western
Germany are particularly interested in a rapid development
of socialist democracy in the USSR or in accelerating the
pace of economic, social and cultural progress in our country.

Thus when Soviet dissidents appeal for support in the Western
countries, they must know exactly to whom they are addressing
their appeals. To us, it is obvious that public opinion in the
Western countries is extraordinarily polarized and reacts in
very different ways to events in the USSR and in the other
socialist countries. In fact, those who are primarily interested
in the development of a truly socialist democracy in our
country are the left-wing forces of the West, in other words
socialist and communist Parties, progressive intellectuals, and
various leftist organizations. Right-wing circles in the West,
on the contrary, exploit any shortcomings in the USSR and
any acts of oppression by the Soviet State for their own
demagogic ends; their aim is not to assist the victory of a
'socialism with a human face' but to discredit both socialism
and communism, and thereby strike a blow above all against
the forces of the Left in their own countries.

Certain of our dissidents sometimes give the impression
that they fully understand this. They transfer their dissatisfaction with the political practice of the CPSU to the whole Left
in the West, and consider that there too a victory of the

Left would yield no more than a new variety of totalitarianism. In their declarations, addresses and protests these dissidents have lately more and more appealed not so much to the Left as to the Right in the Western countries. This orientation offers no hope for the future, although, of course, every Soviet citizen should be free to choose his own political convictions and sympathies.

Trade: An Example of the Limits of External Powers

It is well known that the 1972 grain harvest in the Soviet Union was very poor. Since no large cereal stocks are available in our country from previous years, there has been a serious dearth of grain for human and animal consumption. This shortage was, however, minimized by unprecedentedly large purchases from the USA, Canada, and a number of other countries. Large consignments of other commodities were also bought abroad. It can naturally be assumed that if Western businessmen and governmental agencies had refused to sell grain and other commodities to the USSR, grave supply difficulties would have arisen in our country in 1972-3. This would undoubtedly have increased discontent among the masses, which might have had to be allayed by some kind of political concessions. All this is, of course, mere hypothesis. In any case, it would have become necessary to adopt economic measures to ensure a swifter development of our agriculture. But why on that account would American producers have denied themselves a lucrative deal? From their point of view, why should they give up their profits?

To help to develop Soviet agriculture, or to convert the USSR within a short space of time from an importer of grain, meat, and butter into an exporter of these goods is not the aim of the US farm lobby. Of course, the ruling class in the USA may elect to break economic relations with any country, as it did with Cuba. The purpose of that decision was clear and the loss to US economy from the blockade of Cuba was insignificant. However, if this kind of boycott did not achieve its purpose in the case of Cuba, it would be even more senseless if applied to the USSR, at a time when the development of trade relations with the Soviet Union promises no small advantages to the West. Naturally, trade with the West strengthens the economic position of the USSR. However, the West of course also derives self-interested advantages from it. At present, the Western countries seek to import raw materials from the Soviet Union for their industries—iron ore, timber, oil and gas. The USSR also exports to the West and to Japan various metals and gold bullion. In their turn, the West and Japan export to the USSR various kinds of equipment—mainly, it would seem, for the oil, gas and timber industries, for coalmining and harbour installations—as well as light industrial goods, grains and foodstuffs. Significantly, the Jackson Amendment would make it difficult to import Soviet finished products into the USA, but it would in no way hamper either US exports of equipment or grain to the USSR or imports of Soviet raw materials to the USA. This merely demonstrates once again that the emergence of the USSR on the world market as a strong industrial power, exporting high quality machinery, light industrial products, motor cars or aircraft to the Western countries as well as to the less developed lands, is a prospect which is far from being the dream of Western businessmen.

There are also limits to the efficacy of external pressures from public organizations and press organs. The Western public rightly protests against attempts to deprive a man like Sakharov of the possibility of freely expressing his views, or a writer like Solzhenitsyn of the normal conditions required for literary creation, against the imprisonment of Amalrik or the confinement in psychiatric hospitals of men like Grigorenko, Plyushch and others. On the other hand, no one could insist that Sakharov's declarations or interviews be given fully sympathetic treatment in *Pravada* or *Izvestya*, or that Solzhenitsyn's new novels be praised in *Novy Mir* or *Znamya*. At the same time it cannot be regarded as normal that Soviet citizens should learn of dissidents' statements or artistic works only from foreign broadcasts and newspapers. We have already had occasion to propose that some institutional machinery should be set up in our country for a dialogue with the various dissenting groups.

The Dangers of Russo-Centrism

At present public opinion in the West reacts much more sharply and actively to negative events in the USSR than it did 15 or 35 years ago. Nevertheless, it would be an illusion to think that the Western public will become more preoccupied by the internal problems of the USSR than by those within their own countries. In this respect we do not consider that Solzhenitsyn's strictures in his address 'Peace and Violence' are just. However important external pressure, in the last analysis the fundamental problems of any country and especially of large powers such as the USSR, can only be resolved by the people and government of that country.

Solzhenitsyn writes: 'Could a Negro militant in South Africa be detained and tormented with impunity for four years as General Grigorenko has been? The storm of world indignation would have torn the roof off his prison long ago'. This position is mistaken. In the same address we find no such strong words of protest, of which Solzhenitsyn is so capable, against the odious apartheid system in South Africa. Unfortunately, no protests have yet torn the roofs off the prisons and camps where hundreds of thousands of South African blacks are incarcerated. No protests have yet flung open the gates of the concentration camps in Indonesia where hundreds of thousands are held without trial for their left-wing beliefs. No protests have yet halted the bloody terror in Chile. Of course, one's own pain always seems worse than that of others. Nevertheless, it is impermissible to fall into a kind of 'Moscow-Centrism' and fail to see that in many other countries there are political problems just as acute and very often even more acute than those of the USSR.

The Short-term and Long-term Prospects for Détente

Global international détente, just as the lessening of tension in any area of the world, depends on the governments and leaders in power at this particular time. It is evident that at present the Soviet government is greatly interested in relaxing international confrontation and developing external co-operation and trade. To achieve these aims it is prepared to make certain concessions which it would not have contemplated a few years ago. The major Western countries are also prepared to make many concessions. Nevertheless, in neither case should important concessions on internal policy be expected. It would therefore be unrealistic and wrong for the West to deliver any ultimatum that the USSR should fulfil certain preconditions for diplomatic détente and economic co-operation. We believe that détente, co-operation, trade, and tourism are important benefits in themselves. More often than not, it is unreasonable to pose preconditions in negotiating these questions. For it is surely plain that in the past the high pitch of international tension drained the strength of the great powers by a futile arms race, and diverted their enormous resources away from the development of their productive potential into the accumulation of unprecedented means of destruction.

Hitherto the détente has not led to any enlargement of democratic liberties in the USSR; on the contrary, it has been used by certain groups to tighten suppression of dissent. However, in a more distant future—although this may not be a very comforting prognosis—détente will undoubtedly contribute to the extension of democratic rights and liberties in our country. For it is precisely in periods of détente that the efficacy of public opinion grows considerably in shaping the internal affairs of each major power. By contrast, a country which is isolated and cut off from the outside world by various Cold War barriers becomes insensitive to protests and views beyond its frontiers. We can see the truth of this not only in the case of great powers, but even in the case of little Albania. In this sense, it must be said that the relaxation of international tension is in itself a very important pre-condition, though not the only one, for the development of democracy in Soviet society. For this reason, we believe that Brandt was justified to state that he would advocate détente even if Stalin were still in power.

In conclusion, we would repeat that no matter how significant the pressure of progressive international opinion may be, the prime impulse towards democratization in the USSR must necessarily come from within Soviet society itself, including its present and future leaders. The present regressive trends in our domestic political life are, of course, a disquieting symptom. But they do not in any way preclude the emergence of other trends and other situations, whose outlines are difficult to foresee now. During the last fifteen to twenty years a new generation has grown up in the USSR and with it a new levy of leaders, a significant number of whom may prove capable of an outlook on the problems and prospects of development that differs from that of the leaders of the outgoing generation.

It is clear that a majority of our leaders now increasingly understands that it is intolerable that the Soviet Union should lag so far behind the capitalist countries in the *material living standards* of its population—the production of the basic necessities of life for our people. Some effective steps have already been taken to remedy this. But the level of our production of spiritual values is extremely low, although the majority of Soviet people precisely regards spiritual nourishment as an ever more important component of their needs. At the same time it is obvious that without true democracy, without a free exchange of ideas and opinions, it is absolutely impossible to create any satisfactory spiritual values. Let us hope that in time all Soviet people, including the majority of their leaders, will make this simple truth their own.

November 1973

How might a thaw be brought about?

Those who oppose the bureaucratic regime in the USSR have in common only demands for elementary democratic rights and notably the right to leave the country. The Western Press puts a spotlight on the declarations of those who seek the support of capitalist powers, such as Sakharov, so as by such pressure to seek observance of the Human Rights Declaration of the United Nations, or Solzhenitzyn seeking a return to the past in which he believes after the style of a Russian 'old believer'. The Western Press largely passes over in silence the writings and declarations of Marxists who oppose the Russian bureaucracy.

As for the Soviet leaders, they do not content themselves with crushing by repression and sending into mental asylums men such as General Grigorenko. They use the old device of lumping together all their opponents—anti-Stalinists or anti-communists —a method that enables them to discredit the whole opposition by fathering on it the reactionary declarations of Solzhenitzyn or the questionable tactics of Sakharov. In this way they use publications abroad to put blame on opponents of the Left in power. At the same time they have to take into account international opinion, particularly opinion on the Left. But it is precisely the press of the Left which really carries information on repression against revolutionaries. Yet even the organ of the Unified Socialist Party in France, the *Tribune Socialiste* has up till now shown extreme discretion on this subject, despite the fact that comrades on the Left have been active on this matter. At root, the Left fears that it may put off its communist allies if it deals with such dangerous topics, and it only does so when the big press has determined some definite trend of opinion, as over Solzhenitzyn. This is a very dangerous view to take of united action. What happens to Soviet revolutionaries is much more than a question of the individuals involved. To allow them to be crushed without reacting strongly, is to open the way to a peculiar sort of socialist society.

But Medvedev is not content just to put an end to this lumping together of opponents. He calls it to mind that only an international détente can bring about a thaw in the USSR.

Quite specifically it is not just a change in climate that is at issue—on the contrary, those who presently champion the détente in the Communist Party of the Soviet Union can only do so so long as they demand guarantees to the 'Stalinists' against any relaxation which might result in the structure of bureaucratic absolutism. That is why, paradoxically, détente has up to now brought about a reinforcement of restrictive measures.

The positive role of the détente is a longer term one. General participation of the USSR in the world market will bring about scientific exchanges, cultural exchanges and exchanges of tourists which will undermine the monopoly that the bureaucracy has at present in information and ideas. The dynamic of this situation is in fact the same as that at work when the world market was developing in the early days of capitalism. The Soviet bureaucracy has been able to avoid the impact of the world market thanks to the barriers with which it has surrounded the development of State capitalism. Today these barriers become the main obstacle, not only to evolution towards a social-ist society (which is not at all what the Soviet leaders are after) but also to scientific and technical development and hence to economic progress and any new improvement in the standard of life.

The conflicts that divide Soviet leading circles relate to this contradiction between economic development and the mainten-ance of the general restrictions with which the country is weighed down by the bureaucratic system. It is in the higher circles of the political and economic administration that these conflicts occur as of now. On this topic Medvedev's analysis is somewhat scanty because he makes his analysis in political and, curiously, parlia-mentary terms. He finds there opposition between the 'rightists' (partisans of total restraint and isolation) and the progressive elements in the administration of the Soviet Communist Party. In fact this is a social conflict in the first instance. The technocrats demand an orientation towards consumer goods, optimal use of scientific and economic resources—and hence at least a partial lifting of commercial and financial barriers. The bureaucracy, which has to reckon with the aspirations of the masses for a higher standard of life, is divided as to what concessions are possible and what safeguards ought to go with them.

They fear seeing developments getting out of their control, as has happened in Yugoslavia, to a certain extent, and as almost happened in Poland and in Czechoslovakia. In Czechoslovakia, the technocrats had looked for support from the working class. To win them as allies, they had woken the working class quite suddenly from its apparent passivity and had opened the way to a social revolution. There was nothing accidental about the fact that the main repressive measures were taken in 1968.

In the USSR, to be sure, the situation is not the same as in Czechoslovakia. There is a monopoly of information and of ideological development in the hands of a bureaucracy which also has a monopoly control over jobs; this has brought about a deep depoliticization of the masses who for some generations now have become used to carrying out orders. The working class is politically disintegrated. All opposition is atomized. More than that, the manner in which their outlook has been shaped ideologically makes them see not merely the mildest hint of opposition and openness but the slightest expression of a personal view as an attack on the society in which they live.

These facts point to the limits that must be put on hopes for a thaw. When a proletarian force acquires a separate existence in the USSR, it will not, to be sure, be able to avoid allying itself in the first instance with the technocracy against the bureaucracy. This is the state of affairs which tends to make the intelligentsia the most frequent recruiting ground for the opposition.

For the time being, revolutionaries, in the USSR, can only count on methods that are strange to them.

Things would go ahead in a different way if a proletarian revolution developed in Europe. That is why the Soviet bureaucracy is so fearful of any course of events which might lead to a revolution in France. It did everything it could to prevent the victory of the 'Union de la Gauche' behind its common programme. Diplomats from countries of Eastern Europe came together in Paris to work everything that lay within their power to help Giscard win the day. On the eve of the election, the Soviet Ambassador publicly declared that he would be personally satisfied with a victory for Giscard. The French Communist Party could not do otherwise than protest publicly at this.

All the evidence points to the fact that the Soviet bureaucracy was afraid, as in 1968, that a victory of the left might unleash a mass movement of the people threatening the capitalist order. There is nothing that would help the Soviet workers more than a revolution in Europe.

Reflections on Roy Medvedev's 'Democratization and Détente'

Roy Medvedev's essay on 'Democratization and Détente' is thought-provoking and stimulating. It explicitly and implicitly poses a number of problems which, like a chain reaction, produce further questions touching, in their turn, on a multitude of others.

In his book *De La Démocratie Socialiste* Medvedev gave a survey of various currents of opinion among the Soviet Party intelligentsia. In that context he described himself as belonging to the current of the democratic left whose ideological sources lie in Marxism-Leninism. However, Medvedev and his co-thinkers do not treat the tenets of Marxism-Leninism as Holy Writ or as Gospel beyond criticism or change; they want to adapt it to modern needs and conditions, created by the development of science and technology. They also demand the return to Leninist norms in the Party and State, and press for a thorough democratization of party life and of society at large.

As if to dispel our illusions and wishful thinking, Medvedev, time and again, in the essay and in the book, warns that all political currents within the framework of Marxism and outside it involve 'only a minimal fraction of the Soviet intelligentsia'; that 'the protests are made by individuals or at best by very small groups of people . . .'; and that even this 'minimal fraction' has dwindled in recent years as result of renewed repression and attacks on dissenters. The dissenters, cruelly persecuted as they are, can derive some wry satisfaction seeing how threatening their activity seemed to be to the authorities and how it alarmed at least the Right wing among the ruling bureaucracy. Nevertheless, 'the forces of the progressive intelligentsia are still too feeble' to overcome the recent neo-Stalinist tendencies in

Soviet political life; and they are certainly 'too feeble' to effect any fundamental change such as the return to 'Leninist norms'.

What is perhaps even more distressing is to watch how under the blows from obtuse and dull-witted authorities, some dissenters themselves abandon their 'progressive tendencies': isolated, cut off from the sources of unbiased information, deprived of any group support and of any possibility to develop, test, and clarify their ideas in debates with like-minded friends, they express, as Medvedev says, more and more extremist points of view and put forward 'less and less constructive proposals, being moved more by emotion than by the considerations of political efficacity'. This remark testifies to Medvedev's admirable insight into the psychological reaction to persecution: driven to despair, people react in a desperate manner; and we have had quite a few new examples of this emotional (and perhaps even thoughtless) reaction since Medvedev wrote his essay.

*   *   *

It seems that the crux of the whole problem of the democratization of the USSR is summed up in the following passage of Medvedev's essay: '. . . the forces of the progressive intelligentsia are still too feeble to oppose the sharp swing to the right in our political and social life. It is also necessary to take into account the political passivity of the working class, of the employees, and even more so of the peasantry'. From here Medvedev goes on to postulate a change from 'above' supported from 'below'. In other words, we are faced with the question: Who is going to be the main agent of the change of the Soviet regime?

Marxists had always expected the industrial workers to be the most dynamic force in the capitalist society, the main agents of socialist revolution. In 1917 and for a short period afterwards, the Russian workers justified that expectation. Where then lies this dynamic force in the post-revolutionary and post-capitalist society? It has been pointed out that all over the Soviet bloc— in East Germany in 1953, in Hungary in 1956, in Poland in 1956 and in 1970, and in Czechoslovakia after Novotny—it was the pressure from below that brought about changes (albeit too shortlived). And yet this pressure from below was stimulated or initiated from above: the liberalization of the USSR after Stalin's death, after the 20th Congress, was the first breach in the glacis of the Stalinized regimes. Maybe Stalin's heirs learned some wisdom from Alexander II who abolished serfdom. They may have paraphrased his words and decided that it was better to abolish the worst features of Stalinism from above than to wait until they are abolished violently from below. 'The Thaw' after 1956 produced cracks all over the Soviet bloc, but no more than cracks. In Czechoslovakia, for instance, the reaction to 1956 was longer delayed than in any other country. What, however, burst the cracks of the Czech glacis much wider in 1968 was 'the initiative from above', from some progressive elements in the ruling party, combined with the consistent and revolutionary pressure from below. Given the slightest chance, the masses erupted on to the political scene and from the 'object' of politics became the 'subject' of the process of democratization. Four months after the fall of Novotny from the top of the hierarchical ladder, spontaneously, at its base sprang into being genuine Workers' Councils embracing nearly half the industrial enterprises and at least 800,000 workers. Thus was realized true democratic self-management, the direct participation of the producers in the affairs immediately affecting their interests and their lives. Thus also 'liberalization' opened the way to democratization.

The revolt of the Polish workers in the Baltic ports in 1970 was also an action from below, which resulted in the changes high above: in the fall of Gomulka and the arrival of the new General Secretary Gierek. One should not forget that Gomulka himself was brought to power in 1956 by popular acclaim. This was the Polish 'Spring of the Peoples': workers spontaneously poured out into the streets and were joined by students and professors, poets and philosophers. Yes, great hopes were aroused. Fourteen years later Gomulka was dismissed from his post to appease the dockers and shipworkers of Gdynia, Elblag and Szczecin, who at first struck against the sharp rise in the cost of living. It was the overreaction of the authorities who gave orders to shoot, and not any encouragement from above, that spurred the workers to further action, to further more fundamental demands and finally to force the changes at the top of the hierarchy.

Can one find, in the Polish events, and even more so in the Czechoslovak experience of 1968, any pointers to the possible developments inside the Soviet Union? Yes and no. What happened in Poland and Czechoslovakia revealed to us a great deal about the atmosphere in these countries. It was as if a curtain was raised and a shaft of light thrown on the stage where the actors wanted to be seen and understood by all, eager for audience participation. We know much less about the mass of the Soviet workers, about their state of mind, their frustrations and satisfactions and grievances and about the degree of their social consciousness.

It is a tragic paradox that the same working class which in 1917 astonished the world by its energy, political intelligence, and organizational ability, now seems mute and prostrate. It is the same working class and yet not the same. Today it seems to suffer some sort of a collective amnesia which has wiped out of its memory a whole historical period. While all over Eastern Europe the tradition of pre-war class struggles and war-time struggle against the foreign occupation is still alive, in Russia this tradition seems to be extinct, or at best hazy. In 1917 two decades of Marxist propaganda, fresh memories of the struggles of 1905, 1912, 1914, and the Bolsheviks' singleness of purpose had prepared the workers for their role. They took the socialist aim of the revolution for granted. Do they now, six decades later, ever attempt to confront the aim with the achievement?

'The political passivity of our population "below" is . . . obvious', says Medvedev. And further: 'People have learnt to become so silent, and have acquired such a sense of guilt . . .' And yet the same passive masses carry in them, according to Medvedev and many other witnesses of the Russian scene, a powerful dynamic charge of discontent and dissatisfaction. Moreover, most dissenters, not only those on the Right, but even those of the Left, regard this dynamic charge as extremely dangerous for the whole society.

In his grimly Orwellian 'Will the Soviet Union survive till 1984?' Andrei Amalrik foresees that any slow-down in the growth of prosperity of the broad Soviet masses would provoke such an outburst of dissatisfaction and violence as would have previously been impossible. He maintains that even the word 'freedom' is understood by the majority as synonymous with the word 'disorder', as 'meaning the possibility of throwing oneself with impunity into anti-social and dangerous activities'. Medvedev trusts that slow as the economic progress of the Soviet Union is, 'it is nevertheless sufficient to avert any uncontrollable growth of dissatisfaction among broad masses of the people'.

From the analyses of Medvedev and the dissenters who stand far to the Right of him, we have an uncanny feeling that the Soviet Union is in some sort of an impasse: the intelligentsia is too feeble to effect a change; the masses are apathetic, yet carry within them a potential of violence too destructive to allow them to rebuild a positive, viable new social order. And so we return again to the fundamental question: to which social stratum can we look for effective agents of further democratization? Who is to control—and by what means—this 'uncontrollable growth of dissatisfaction' among people? Surely, dissatisfaction is and has always been the *primum mobile* of all progress. In order to assure that the dissatisfaction does not remain merely destructive and does not lead only to complete chaos, the apathetic masses must, as in the pre-1917 period learn the pristine ideas of Marxism and Leninism; they must re-learn freedom; they must realize that the identification of Stalinism with socialism was the greatest fraud that Stalin perpetrated not only on the Russian proletariat, that in the name of socialism he pursued policies violating the very spirit of socialism and so compromised the great idea in the eyes of the working classes of the world.

Medvedev's reasoning is clear and convincing, when he argues that 'Under present conditions . . . Marxism can only retain its influence on the consciousness of the people—let alone increase it—by an uncompromisingly honest, open, and truthful scientific analysis of the totality of contemporary social problems and of the whole unfalsified history of international events and revolutionary experience'. Yes, this is all too true. The question is where will this scientific analysis come from? And how is it to break through the crust of apathy and reach the masses? Is not that part of the Soviet intelligentsia which is politically involved —and Marxist—and active too small and too feeble to undertake this task? How to awaken the masses? How to bring such a scientific analysis to the de-politicized worker under the watchful eye of the ubiquitous and hostile State apparatus? Isn't the Marxist scientific analysis of the past, an 'uncompromisingly honest, open and truthful' analysis, just what the bureaucracy fears most? Where then lies hope?

Since Stalin's death, since the 20th and 22nd Congresses, the Soviet bureaucracy can no longer be viewed as one monolithic bloc. Both the Party and the State bureaucracy emerge from all accounts as a group of individuals subjected to similar strains, stresses, tensions, disagreements and antagonisms which are the lot of ordinary mortals. Medvedev, perhaps the best informed observer, speaks about 'polemical disputes and factional struggles within the higher echelons of the Central Committee of the Party'. At the other end of the political spectrum, Amalrik admits that in a moderate form the liberal ideologies of the intelligentsia 'penetrate even into the circles close to the regime'. Maximov, who in his novel *Seven Days of Creation* denounced virulently the whole revolutionary period and the Bolshevik Party right from its inception, yet maintains that 'a movement of reform within the Soviet Communist Party in all probability exists'.

The concrete experience of Czechoslovakia in the first half of 1968 confirms the view that perhaps it is not quite right to damn the Party wholesale and *en bloc*. One should not forget that in Czechoslovakia the first impulse for a change came—unexpectedly—from within the Party in power: the differentiation within the hierarchy of the party and its division into a 'progressive' and 'retrograde' wing proved real enough to produce what Jiri Pelikan had once called a 'palace coup', which resulted in the 'dethronement' of Novotny. Those who are inclined to view the party with all its tendencies, currents and crosscurrents not as a mirror of society (even if somewhat distorting), but as an irredeemable monolithic abomination, ascribe the fiasco of the Prague Spring precisely to the fact that it was brought about in some measure from 'above'. To see

that there is a *non sequitur* in such an argument, it is enough
to ask: Would the Russians have refrained from invading
Czechoslovakia if the stimulus for a radical break with the
past came from outside the Party? The answer is obvious. The
Warsaw Pact armies would have received the order to march
on Prague no matter from which quarter the stimulus for
democratization had come. Heavy tanks and soldiers' boots
had to crush the first shoots of freedom before it was too late,
before they blossomed, before their intoxicating fragrance
spread to other countries still in the grip of Stalinist or neo-
Stalinist winter.

'Any shift towards a more consistent democratization', says
Medvedev, 'is at present possible . . . only as result of certain
initiatives from "above" supported from "below", but not as
a simple result of pressure from "below".' This statement,
coming as it does, from an observer who feels the pulse of his
country and is extremely sensitive to it, has to be accepted as
valid. It begs, however, many questions. We have been warned
from all sides that 'sheer pressure from below' may lead to
an uncontrollable outburst of dissatisfaction among the masses,
prevent a peaceful transition to democratic socialism, produce
results opposite to those that were intended, and endanger
the security of the whole country. But to what degree would
those 'below' have confidence in the initiatives from 'above'?
Would they not view with suspicion any move coming from
a subservient and compromised Party or even from those on
the periphery of it? And how to define at what point an 'outburst' becomes 'uncontrollable'? And who—scientists, managers,
technocrats, historians?—can be entrusted with controlling the
pressure from below? And by what criteria should this control
be exercised and how far should it go? It is futile even to try
and answer these questions from London or Paris. Here we
can only pose them or discuss them in purely theoretical terms.

Some years ago it was fashionable hotly to debate whether
the Left in the West should opt for a reformist or a revolutionary way of struggle against the Soviet bureaucracy. Such
a debate seemed to me irrelevant and presumptuous. Para-
phrasing Engels, one might say that the emancipation of the

Soviet people will be the work of the Soviet people themselves. Medvedev rightly says that 'the prime impulse towards democratization . . . must necessarily come from within the Soviet society'. This does not mean, however, that the Left should stand aside and confine itself to watching passively and mutely the turbulent Soviet scene. No, on the contrary; it should give the strongest support to Soviet Marxists, to the Left wing dissidents with whom it has ideologically so much in common; it should become more and not less active in defending the persecuted dissenters instead of leaving this task to the scribes of reactionary journalism and Pharisaic American Senators not in the least concerned with real democratic freedoms in the USSR.

*   *   *

Contrary to Medvedev's expectations, the 'successes of Soviet foreign policy' and the lowering of international tension have not so far led to any enlargement of democratic liberties in the Soviet Union. This may be so in the short run. If we look somewhat further back into the past, we cannot fail to notice that the darkest period of Russian life coincided with international tension, with hostility of the outside world and the danger of war. To give only two examples: freedom was most cruelly suppressed in Russia during the rise of Nazism—at the time of the Great Purges. It was stifled and trampled upon during the cold war—it was then that Stalin produced his macabre spectacle of the so-called Doctors' Plot. To such horrors Russia has not returned. The recent détente did not bring with it any *consistent* enlargement of civil liberties, and the reason for this should perhaps be sought in the inconsistency and lack of cohesion of the ruling group which tends to take two steps back and one step forward (or two steps forward and one step back) regardless of its foreign policy (which, by the way, lacks consistency too). The détente which we have witnessed in recent years was, so to say, engineered from very high 'above': by capitalist oligarchies in the West and bureaucratic oligarchy in the East. This allows both to boast of their diplomatic and commercial successes; it bolsters their popularity and makes them feel safer and more secure in their saddles. To avert an economic slump, Nixon needs trade and markets in the East, just as the Russians need foreign imports to keep their people below the boiling point of discontent. None of them act in the interest of freedom and genuine democracy, which for both oligarchies is perhaps equally dangerous.

*   *   *

A wise historian once said that the world is 'something like a system of interconnected vessels where the level of freedom and critical thinking tends to even out'. It is not so much the formal treaties and agreements ceremoniously signed at diplomatic banquets that will 'enlarge liberties' in Russia and elsewhere. It is the growth of socialist consciousness, the critical thinking of the Left, the tenacity, vigour and energy with which it will oppose its own repressive oligarchies, that will give encouragement and help the forces of progress and true socialism in the USSR and in the countries where the 'Soviet model' of socialism still prevails.

*   *   *

At the time when Stalin's body was evicted from the Mausoleum on the Red Square and his statue brought down with a crash in one of the squares of Budapest, a prominent editor of a great bourgeois paper remarked wistfully: 'Now we may have to raise monuments to Stalin. Without Stalin the Soviet Union may indeed become so much more attractive to our own working classes that we shall face dangers infinitely more real and threatening than those we had to face during his reign of terror'. Medvedev understands this seeming paradox perfectly well, but some of his fellow-dissenters, who pin their hopes on the American Congress or on Messrs Heath, Wilson, Nixon, or Giscard d'Estaing, don't.

June 1974

The Social Forces behind Détente

We cannot resolve the problem of the inter-relation between the so-called 'process of international détente' and the possibility of a return to genuine socialist democracy in the USSR, if we consider these concepts as divorced from real social forces, based on concrete material interests.

There does not exist any such thing as the 'world leaders' or the 'great power leaders' wishing to avoid increased tensions dangerous for world peace. There exist social groups in power in the USA, in the Soviet Union, or in any other country or group of countries in the world, which make certain moves on the international scene as a function of the interests which they defend.

If the leaders of American imperialism have apparently modified their 'cold war' approach towards the Soviet Union, this is not because they have now adopted an option in favour of 'peaceful coexistence' ('under the pressure of their peoples favourable to the cause of peace'). It is because they have a certain number of short-range goals to attain. Increased international inter-imperialist competition, coupled with increasingly explosive economic contradictions, made *de facto* exclusion of American capital from the slowly growing export markets to the Soviet Union counter-productive from the point of view of the big US monopolies. Likewise, US imperialism has some interest in receiving greater support from Soviet diplomacy in its endeavours to eliminate some of the 'trouble spots' in the semi-colonial countries, like the Cuban-supported guerrilla movements in many Latin-American countries, the Palestinian resistance, or the Indochinese revolution.

From a long-term point of view, there exists a genuine common interest of the ruling circles in the USA, in the USSR and, in fact, in *all* countries, to prevent the arms race from 'getting out of hand', i.e. from rushing into such an accelerated use of sophisticated equipment that the cost would become unbearable even for the richest country in the world. That's what SALT is all about.

The *reality* of *détente*—as opposed to its myth—is therefore limited to these extremely narrow results, which modify only in a very marginal and, indeed, insignificant way, the world situation as it has existed in the last decades.

The cold war in its fundamental sense, which is to say, the arms race between the imperialist bloc and the so-called socialist countries, continues more than ever. In fact, military budgets increase year after year, *détente* notwithstanding. Imperialist and Soviet armed forces continuously jockey for positions, in the Indian Ocean, in the Middle East, in the Mediterranean, in Europe. There are no signs of the relaxation of the abiding basic antagonism between two basically different social systems. As for the myth of a 'two-big-power-conspiracy-for-world-domination', which precisely tries to forget the basic social antagonism between the capitalist and the non-capitalist states, it is contradicted day after day by the realities of the world armaments race, of world politics, and of world conflicts.

Likewise, if the leaders of the Soviet Union meet Nixon (and are ready to give him some modest but real help on the Indochinese and the *Watergate* fronts), this has nothing to do with a 'progressive' option in favour of 'peaceful coexistence' as against 'reactionaries' favouring 'aggression'. They also have some concrete tangible short-term advantages in mind, the uppermost being a better access to Western technology, in order partially to overcome the dangerous tendencies of a slowdown of economic growth in their country. But this does not mean that they are ready to stop the arms race, to dismantle the state monopoly of foreign trade, to give away an inch of the territory which they control directly or indirectly since the end of World War II. It is ludicrous to think that they would be ready to collaborate with Western capitalism for such purposes.

This does not mean that socialists in the West should start 'denouncing' détente or should prefer even more resources to be wasted on the arms race than are already wasted today. The cause of socialist revolution in the capitalist countries, in the same way as the cause of establishing soviet democracy in the 'Eastern bloc' (which revolutionary Marxists call the cause of political revolution), does not depend upon or call for military confrontations between rival big powers. Revolutionists would already be very satisfied if the existing states would *abstain* from using their military establishments in a counter-revolutionary manner, a situation which is not likely to be achieved in any foreseeable future. Even on this very limited field, the Chilean example confirms that 'détente' is of little or no avail. Should tomorrow a 'Prague' spring repeat itself in another Eastern European country, the Soviet bureaucracy would likewise behave in the same way as it did in 1968, 'détente' notwithstanding.

Therefore, it was and remains an unfounded illusion to believe that this sort of 'détente'—a diplomatic manoeuvre strictly controlled by the ruling class in the USA and the ruling social stratum in the Soviet Union—could in any way whatsoever favour a 'process of democratization' inside that country. Historically, one could even make a case for the opposite thesis. Each time the rulers of the Soviet Union have been ready to have closer economic relations with Western capitalism, they tend to increase repression in their own country, in order to avoid a 'spill-over' from the sphere of 'economic liberalization' into the sphere of political 'democratization'.

At the root of the problem there is the question of the nature of the leading group inside the Soviet Union, the reasons for its opposing the 'democratization' process, the *rationale* of its obstinate and consistent clinging to its power monopoly, even at the cost of seriously weakening the economic, political, cultural, and therefore also military, strength of its own country. In the same way as it is impossible to view 'détente' simply as a result of conflicts or combinations of political ideas, it is impossible to understand the nature of the 'power elite' in the Soviet Union simply as a question of people unable to break with outmoded 'ideas', because of 'dogmatic' or 'conservative education' (under Stalin) or psychological blocks against 'progress'.

The rulers of the Soviet Union form a tightly-knit social group, which for lack of a better definition we call 'the bureaucracy' i.e. the sum total of all those who participate in the monopoly of power administration at whatever level of society. This monopoly in the exercise of power entails important material social privileges, which underpin the knitting together of that social layer. Although they are *not* a new social class, have none of the basic characteristics of social classes in history, have no ideology of their own, and form historically a parasitic formation on the body of the wage-earning class (the proletariat), without proper objectively necessary roots in the social relations of production, and without property rights to the means of production, they are quite conscious of their specific material interests, and defend them tooth and nails against all their adversaries.

A 'genuine socialist democracy', as Roy Medvedev so aptly states, is the 'most important precondition for an acceleration of the economic, political, social and cultural development' of the USSR, the absolute prerequisite which 'can give birth to the new motor forces that are necessary to restore health and life to the whole system of Soviet institutions and organizations'. It so happens that such a 'genuine socialist democracy' can only function on the basis of democratically planned and democratically centralized self-management organs in the factories, the offices, the neighbourhoods, the state and service institutions. It so happens that such a system of democratically planned self-management means the widest possible range of *public* control, *public* discussion, *mass* activity, in every single sphere of social life. This is unthinkable without unfettered freedom of political debate, opposition, contest and organization, i.e. a soviet multi-party system. And this is unthinkable without a public discovery and denunciation of all the illegal and 'legal' sources of material privileges of the bureaucracy, by genuine power organs of the working class, of democratically elected soviets. These privileges would not survive six months of socialist democracy. They would be swept away. There, and not in the sphere of ideology or psychology, is the explanation for the USSR leaders' obstinate resistance to soviet democracy.

It is interesting to note that in the field of economic management, *both* wings of the bureaucracy—the 'liberal' wing which favours more market mechanisms, and the 'conservative' wing which favours bureaucratic centralization—are likewise and consistently opposed to genuine workers' control. Under a 'socialist market economy', workers do not control their destiny any more than under the Stalinist type of bureaucratic centralization. Social inequality and oppression can and do flourish under both variants of bureaucratic rule. If the first has 'advantages' over the second, from the point of view of the working class, it is only because it allows a higher degree of organizational possibility for workers' self-defence and workers' resistance, *against* those who run the economy independently from the proletariat. It leads to greater social and political differentiation—including the appearance of more outspoken proponents of a return to capitalism—but simultaneously it makes the proletariat politically more articulate and more capable of self-organization and self-defence.

For these reasons, illusions in 'reforms from above' in the Soviet Union are as unfounded as illusions in 'détente'. Reforms from above, like those granted in the late fifties, are concessions made by the ruling caste in order to defend and perpetuate its privileges and its power monopoly, not in order to liquidate these privileges or to transform itself into benign 'servants of the people'.

One could say that such reforms, however partial and inadequate, objectively assist a process of slow rebirth of political consciousness and activity of broader social layers, including the working class. This is of course true. But the real dialectics between 'reforms from above' and 'movement from below' are much more complex. More radical 'reforms from above' would require a bigger 'pressure from below', i.e. would appear as *results* rather than *causes* of mass movements. Likewise, 'reforms from above' which would tend to precipitate mass movements dangerous for the survival of the bureaucracy's rule and privileges, which would then be precipitately abolished. The history of tsarism offers many illuminating variants and comments on this type of dialectic.

Medvedev correctly stresses the one key factor in Soviet society which has up till now consistently distorted this dialectic. The most disastrous result of Stalinism, worse even than all the institutions of political repression and terror—although in part a function of these—is the huge process of depolitization of the Soviet working class. This class, which represents, together with the American working class, the numerically largest sector of the world proletariat, has today an extremely low level of political interest and consciousness, although it tenaciously clings to whatever tangible remains of the conquests of the October revolution survive in its eyes, not the least of which is the much higher level of job security and the much lower work rhythm than that which exists in capitalist countries.

It is the absence of a conscious intervention of the Soviet working class in political life which enables 'dissent' to appear as a purely intellectual affair, and which likewise fosters inside the dissenting *intelligentsia* not only one wing of clearly anti-socialist, reactionary thought, but also in general a patronizing and bureaucratic attitude towards the workers. This is evident in the writings of Solzhenitsyn. It is also partially present in Medvedev's *essay*.

Again we are faced here with a dialectical and not a simply linear-causal relationship. Despairing of the 'passive' and 'apolitical' mass, Medvedev pins all his hopes for initiating change on 'reforms from the top'. But as long as the mass remains 'passive', these 'reforms from the top' are condemned to remain marginal, as the last two decades have confirmed. You cannot 'guide' a mass to cease being 'passive'; it can only break with passivity by becoming active. This in turn calls for a fundamental reorientation of the Marxist dissenters (the others will not help in this field): towards assisting the mass of the workers in again becoming politically active and conscious. As long as they do not look for ways and means in that direction, 99% of the political endeavours of Marxist dissenters in the Soviet Union will in the end be of no avail.

'Socialist democracy' means in the first place *self*-government, *self*-administration and *self*-management by the *mass* of the workers. In the same way as you cannot learn to swim outside the water, you cannot be led towards the road of self-management and self-administration by benign, well-wishing patronizers, who continue to decree from above 'what is best for the (passive, a-political, ignorant) mass'. *Self organization of the workers' struggles today is a necessary precondition for self-management of a socialist society tomorrow.* It is in that direction that the Marxist dissenters in the Soviet Union have to turn. It is a difficult and dangerous road, undoubtedly. But it is the only road which will lead to a genuine rebirth of soviet democracy, of real soviet power.

Basically, Soviet workers are 'a-political' because Stalin and Stalinism have discredited communism and Marxism and no tangible alternative exists for them. Capitalism they instinctively reject, and rightly so. Stalinist 'socialism' they cannot accept. What should they turn to? What should they fight for?

The greatest contribution socialists in the West can therefore make towards a rebirth of socialist democracy in the USSR, lies neither in their advocating 'détente', nor in their defence of the Soviet dissenters against repression (although this last task is absolutely indispensable and must be pursued relentlessly, in favour of *all* of them, irrespective of their right or wrong ideology. Without free political debate in the USSR, a rebirth of Marxism and of working class consciousness is unthinkable in that country). It lies in the struggle for a socialist revolution which will show in practice that another 'model' of a non-capitalist economy and society (of 'building socialism') is possible, than that of the Soviet Union, a model in which the degree of political and individual freedom, and especially of self-determination of the worker in his daily productive and social activity, is immensely higher than that which exists under bourgeois democracy. Such a 'model' would more than anything else help the Soviet workers to act politically and so implement socialist democracy at home.

We are convinced that such a society would enjoy likewise a much higher degree of economic efficiency, of social and material welfare, of capacity to reorganize technology and the contents of work in a creative and ecological equilibrium-preserving manner, than the most advanced capitalist countries know today. Therefore we say that the real twin processes to cure the world's evils are not a fake 'détente' and an illusionary 'democratization from above', but a socialist revolution in the capitalist countries, triggering off and intertwined with anti-bureaucratic mass movements, above all of the working class, in the USSR.

Solidarity is Indivisible

'In fact, those who are primarily interested in the development of a truly socialist democracy in our country are the left wing forces of the West.'—Roy Medvedev.

The things a man thinks of make you realize the things he lacks, Goethe once said. Thus the dissenters in the West talk about socialism, while the dissenters in the East talk of democracy. Does this prove what Goethe said? Hardly. The West does have some civil liberties, but it does not have democracy. The East has state ownership, but it does not have socialism. What both lack is socialist democracy.

Why is it so difficult to find common ground between the Left in the West and the opposition in the East? Lately these difficulties have become even more marked. Solzhenitsyn is a case in point. His case has given rise to some questions concerning the attitude of the Left in Western Europe towards dissenting tendencies and currents in the countries of Eastern Europe. Not only do established communist parties point out that any gesture of solidarity with dissenters is likely to be caught up in the tide of anticommunism; this is also a legitimate fear of people and groups in the Left who have no illusions about Solzhenitsyn's home country. Nevertheless this objection seems to us to be a relic from a time when the fight against fascism forced everybody to take either one side or the other. Then Malraux in his novel *L'Espoir* had the Spaniard Manuel say that a revolutionary is a born Manichean: only petty bourgeois intellectuals can take an interest in nuances and general values.

Since then things have changed profoundly. With the exception of the Vietnamese, there does not seem to be a single communist party that has not been accused of anticommunist ideas by another communist party. At the same time in a number of countries groups calling themselves 'communist' have established themselves on the left of the official communist parties and there exists no international licensing office that can stop them from using this brand name. When these, too, in turn are being called 'anticommunist' this only adds to the general loss of meaning of the term. It is not, after all, irrelevant whether you criticise a country because it is socialist or too socialist or whether you criticise it because it is not socialist or not socialist enough.

The same goes for the charge (or the objection) to being caught up in the tide of anticommunism for calling it barbarous when a well-known writer is dispatched out of his country like a mailbag. For one thing, in terms of mere semantics antisovietism is impossible when applied to a country in which the soviets in their original meaning—organs in a direct democracy of producers—no longer exist. But apart from this the very term 'antisoviet' is a term agreed upon at a time of the cold war, when both military blocs were facing each other in confrontation. Today, thinking in terms of blocs will merely lead to blocked thinking. At a time when the Rockefeller Bank has just recently opened a branch in Moscow's Karl Marx Street and negotiations with the Moscow city council about laying out a golf course for American citizens are well under way, the terminology of the cold war needs some adjusting. The superpowers co-operate, but of course they still remain rivals. In some instances this rivalry has its positive aspects as in the carefully dosed aid for Vietnam and the aid for Cuba, given with some ulterior motives. But it would be better to spare us the laboured attempts to glorify this kind of co-operation as a form which the international class struggle is taking.

Solidarity with whom? This is a question often asked by people in the Left. Solidarity with Grigorenko, who sees himself as a Leninist, or with Solzhenitsyn, who degrades Lenin as a forerunner of Stalin? With Medvedev, an avowed Marxist, or with Sakharov, a professed Liberal? Without any doubt these are serious differences which have developed within the opposition groups in the Eastern European countries, manifesting themselves also among the exiles from Czechoslovakia.

It is necessary, however, to reflect on how these attitudes have come about. There is Sakharov, who started out as a Marxist, later calling himself a socialist and has now contented himself with the label of 'Liberal'. Solzhenitsyn was a Marxist as a young man. At the time of his arrest he had appealed to 'true Leninism' and during the Khruschev era in his story *For the Good of the Cause* he spoke about communists fighting against bureaucracy. (What are we to make of a 'society in transition' which leads to this sort of transition in society?) Rudi Dutschke has probably spoken for many left-wing groups when, in the case of Solzhenitsyn, he talked about 'critical solidarity', stressing solidarity as well as disagreement with some of what Solzhenitsyn thinks and says. The term 'critical solidarity' has seen a sort of renaissance since Bert Brecht's 'Arbeitsjournal' was published and it was revealed that the great writer had criticised Stalin's policy, but at the same time—it was in the middle of the war—professed a critical solidarity with the Soviet Union. But the term misses another important set of problems, namely, the responsibility of the Western European Left for some of the things that are now happening within the Soviet opposition. We need not only critical solidarity but also self-criticism in solidarity.

Before 1968 the people who are now called dissidents used to publish their opinions and their material through the correspondents of communist newspapers or through their friends in the leaderships of communist parties in Western Europe. Since 1968 this has stopped. There has been a certain amount of 'normalization' within the communist parties, different in its appearance and in its quality, which nevertheless has led to a state of affairs in which every contact with dissident groups and people in Eastern Europe is now strenuously avoided. Even less is any attempt made to discuss democratic revolutionary alternatives with these groups. The result of this has been an odd kind of democratic schizophrenia: on the one hand everyone is at pains to dissociate themselves from the Russian model of socialism, on the other hand everyone sticks to diplomatic protocol and refuses contact with those who could possibly work out an alternative to this model in their own countries.

This goes for the groups of the New Left, too, with the exception of the Trotskyite groups and 'Il Manifesto' in Italy. In 1968 most of them had a total blackout regarding the Prague Spring. They saw this event solely as a struggle of bureaucrats versus bureaucrats, of technocrats versus technocrats, and entirely missed the fact that the whole future of socialism in Europe was at stake. They did not understand that in the countries of Eastern Europe intellectual liberties are not merely liberties for intellectuals. They did not understand that without a minimum of information and democracy the working class is in danger of being reduced from a 'Klasse an sich', as Karl Marx said, to a 'Klasse für sich'. As a matter of fact there is no demand more revolutionary and more leftward in the countries of Eastern Europe today than the call for freedom of opinion and freedom of thought.

The elementary reaction against affronts to human rights has played an enormous part in the rise of the labour movement. Double-entry bookkeeping concerning the sense of justice has contributed to the fact that today the political, moral and economic crisis of the bourgeoisie coincides with an ideological crisis in the labour movement. The struggle of the labour movement loses its credibility when in a question involving elementary justice silence is advocated as an expression of class consciouness. It is impossible to oppose the disgusting 'Radikalenerlass' (ban on radicals) in the German Federal Republic, it is impossible to voice with any credibility the legitimate protest against the ban on this or that scholar from a university because of his membership in the German CP if at the same time one keeps silent about the fact that in a neighbouring country hundreds of professors and scientists —most of them communists—have lost their chairs and their means of scholarship because the country has lost its independence.

Solidarity is indivisible or else it is not solidarity. Only a revaluation of the morals of socialism can enable us to meet the disquieting developments within the opposition in Eastern Europe mentioned by Medvedev. Solidarity is our strength, Brecht has taught us. The weakness of the Western European Left is in no small way rooted in the fact that for many of its sections solidarity is not indivisible.

One does not have to agree with the general concept of Medvedev. One may regret that in his thinking there is no place for the Soviets in their original form as organs of a democracy of producers. But nevertheless he has recognised that it is necessary to link the opposition in the East with the Left in the West. It is this which makes his opinions vitally important.

Possibilities of Evolution to Democratic Socialism

The main problem posed by Medvedev's text seems to be: what are the prospects for the Soviet Union (and similar political systems) to evolve towards really democratic socialism under the present conditions of lessening international tension?

I think that he is right in holding that while détente 'has been used by certain groups to tighten suppression of dissent', it will, in the long run, contribute to the extension of democratic rights and liberties. It also seems to be true that changes in the direction of democracy in Soviet Union cannot be 'swift' and that one of the decisive factors of the change must be 'struggles at the top' and initiative 'from above'.

The most controversial point in Roy Medvedev's article is, however, his scepticism concerning the possible role of the popular masses and the intelligentsia in the process of democratization. At first he at least concedes that this process in the USSR is possible only as a result of certain initiatives, 'from above, *supported from below*'.[1] But in the subsequent passage he makes a less flexible statement: 'In such conditions a reorganization of social and economic management, an enlargement of political and civic liberties, an expansion of socialist democracy, can come *not* as a result of open pressure by the popular masses and the intelligentsia, but as a consequence of initiatives, "from above".' Medvedev elaborates his view by mentioning, on the one hand, how the population 'below' is passive, silent, obsessed with a sense of guilt, how during the period of 'liberalization' most intellectuals adopted a waiting attitude; on the other hand, how most of the important changes, such as the exposure of the cult of personality of Stalin at the 20th Congress and the thaw after the 22nd Congress, were the work of those occupying positions at the political summits.

Passages like this leave the impression that the fate of social-ism depends almost exclusively on the insight and goodwill of the bureaucracy. But there are also other passages which at least ask good questions. Medvedev says for example 'But if today it is not the outlook of those below that is of decisive importance, but the moods and views of those above, how can the political heights be impelled to proceed not towards a further "tightening of the screws" but towards an enlargement of socialist democracy?'

Indeed, what social forces exist which might impel the political leadership to move in one direction rather than the other?

At the very end of his article Medvedev gives credit to that new generation of leaders who now increasingly understand the need to improve the material living standards of the Soviet people. Then he adds 'But the level of our production of spiritual values is extremely low, although the majority of Soviet people precisely regard spiritual nourishment as an ever more important component of their needs. At the same time it is obvious that without true democracy, without a free exchange of ideas and opinions, it is absolutely impossible to create any satisfactory spiritual values. Let us hope that in time all Soviet people, including the majority of their leaders, will make this simple truth their own.'

We obviously have here a vicious circle. A high level of the production of spiritual values, a new humanist culture, is surely a necessary condition of socialism. This high level is impossible without true democracy. And *vice versa* true democracy is impossible without previous creation of certain spiritual values, without a 'socialist enlightenment'. Where will this new culture come from? Is the only thing to do *to hope* that the leaders might eventually understand that they must introduce socialist democracy in order to ensure a high level of 'spiritual nourish-ment', in order to build up a genuinely socialist society?

But is there any *ground* for such a hope? And is it possible to *do* something in addition to hoping?

One of the most naive and harmful prejudices in the contemporary socialist movement is the view that capitalism must
inevitably be followed by a classless, stateless, marketless, elite-
less society, that therefore the leaders of a contemporary social
revolution, pushed by the iron hand of historical necessity, have
no other choice but to eventually build up such a society.

However, in fact social revolutions clear the ground for the
realization of more than just one historical possibility. In our
time, they mobilize all kinds of non-proletarian social groups,
and their activists and leaders are very different kinds of people,
who are ostensibly guided by the same ideology, but who inter-
pret this ideology in very different ways and are actually motiv-
ated by very different aspirations. What is being described as
'building of socialism' takes place in some societies which have
to go a long way to become industrialized and urbanized, the
political structure of which is below the level of XVIII century
bourgeois democracy, the culture of which is lacking the great
spiritual values of the epoch of the Enlightenment and is still
permeated by authoritarian and patriarchal ideas and attitudes.
Deep below the optimistic rhetoric of the leading cadres there
is a sense of inferiority and insecurity. The new order must be
preserved by force, it cannot offer either the level of material
consumption or of civil liberties prevailing in the surrounding,
supposedly historically inferior, bourgeois world.

What types of leaders can be expected to grow under such
conditions? All types in a large continuum between genuine
revolutionaries, sincerely committed to the cause, over cold
pragmatic rulers who could equally function in any society, to
the ruthless, power-hungry autocrats whose vanity and egoism
have no limits. From the objective conditions will flow any
assessment of how great is the possibility and how much time is
needed to create a genuinely socialist community. From the outcome of the struggle among various factions within the presumably monolithic leadership and especially from the way in which
the popular masses react to existing social conditions and to
initiatives for change—will be determined whether post-revolutionary society can develop into democratic socialism, or des-
potism of the Stalinist variety, or some more liberal form of

state capitalism, or any conceivable mixture of these three. Among various possible types of social change the following three are worth closer consideration: (1) the emergence of a new society as a consequence of the scientific and technological revolution; (2) an anti-bureaucratic political revolution; (3) a series of reforms achieved through the pressure of the popular masses leading to the new society.

(1) The official theory in the Soviet bloc is that communism will inevitably emerge as the result of the scientific and technological revolution. The element of truth in this theory is the fact that the development of the productive forces really does prepare the ground and increase the objective possibilities for the transition toward a more humane and democratic form of social life. But it does not *guarantee* any such transition. A high level of material consumption is compatible with extreme forms of bureaucratism. Catching up with America in wealth and comfort need not involve much progress in socialist democracy. In order to accomplish this task, primitive, uneducated apparatchiks would certainly have to be replaced by highly skilled technicians; the whole process of management could be computerized without transcending its alienated, authoritarian character. While people are passive and apparently satisfied with being ruled, their rulers can hardly be expected to go out of their way and compel them to become free.

(2) Does it follow then that sooner or later the working class must organize a new rebellion, and that the anti-bourgeois revolution must be followed by an anti-bureaucratic one? It does not require a great deal of knowledge and wisdom to come to the conclusion that the task of organizing such a movement is neither very promising nor very practically feasible. It is not feasible because the most elementary conditions for organized political life outside the official political organizations are lacking. It can easily be suppressed in its initial stage because it is forbidden by law; because the law pretends to be a necessary means to protect the new 'socialist' order; because the institutions for enforcing the law are quite powerful and because they can count on the co-operation of vast numbers of informers, both Party members and ordinary citizens for whom

any act of rebellion, illegal conspiracy, or even harmless civil disobedience, is a hostile, counter-revolutionary deed. And even if an organized illegal opposition could survive these initial perils, all the genuinely counter-revolutionary forces outside and inside the country would immediately join and try to use the movement for their own purposes. Such a movement would lack even a minimum of ideological coherence. In another text[2] Roy Medvedev has analyzed the present-day 'Opposition' in the Soviet Union and found the following factions in it: 'Westerners' (who reduce Marxism to Stalinism and fight for a parliamentary democracy), 'Ethical socialists', 'Christian socialists', and 'Legalists' (who fight for greater respect for the law), 'Anarcho-communists' (the extreme Left, which demands the complete abolition of all forms of Stalinism).

But the essential difficulty with an anti-bureaucratic political movement would be its narrowly *political* character. Marx already established in 1844 that 'a revolution of a *political* kind, organizes in accordance with its narrow and discordant outlook, a ruling group in society at the expense of society'.[3] The vanguard of an anti-bureaucratic movement would, in all probability, under the given conditions, become a new bureaucratic elite.

What is in fact required is not a simple political act, a change of government, but a much more complex and profound social change which would make any professional, political, government redundant.

After the successful overthrow of the political power of the bourgeoisie the road to socialism leads through a lasting, mass-scale effort to create a new consciousness, a new culture, a new style of life, to increase participation and self-determination at all social levels, to gradually abolish the remaining old injustices and the new bureaucratic privileges, to create a whole network of new self-governing institutions and producer's associations which would tend to replace the state in the functions of coordination and direction.

To begin with one has to compel the ruling vanguard to stand by its own words. There is a vast gap between revolutionary declarations (Party programmes, constitutions, laws, political platforms) and actual practice. While the merely *political* rebel risks being labelled counter-revolutionary, the social revolutionary exposes the political elite to a similar danger by forcing it to live up to its own programmes, laws, promises. Instead of placing himself outside the law, he urges the full realization of the revolutionary spirit of the new law, placing the bureaucracy into the position of risking the violation of its own legality, of undermining its own legitimacy. The basic presupposition, however, of all post-capitalist development is a genuine cultural revolution: bringing to social consciousness awareness of the historical possibilities of further social change, creation of a new structure of motivation, new hierarchy of needs (involving the overcoming of the artificial needs created by a consumer society), new attitudes of individuals towards their political leaders and institutions of power (overcoming the semi-feudal servility of a humble, obedient subject, *Untertan*). The bourgeois democratic revolution was not possible without the Bourgeois Enlightenment; and the *Socialist democratic revolution* will not be *possible without a Socialist Enlightenment.*

Here the great potential role of Marxist intellectuals becomes evident. They utterly fail when they become mere ideological servants of the new ruling elite. They end in frustration and despair when they preach ideas that find no echo among the general public, ideas that lack mediation with the life experience of the time. They have a chance of becoming active subjects of history when they succeed in mediating between the experiences of many preceding generations, condensed in great works of culture, and the experience of their own generation. Only then are they able to express and articulate some of the most important, vaguely felt general needs and potentialities of the time.[4] New, explicitly stated, ideas cannot simply be impressed into people's consciousness from outside: they have to be recognized and *internalized.*

This reunion of the two powerful factors: the accumulated wisdom of the culture of the great humanist, egalitarian tradition, on the one hand, and the great potential energy of mass movements, on the other—is a necessary condition of any genuine social revolution. If a mass movement cannot take an organized form, for the reasons earlier examined, there are two other forms in which it can be manifested :

One is a sudden, spontaneous explosion like that in Berlin 1953, or those in Poznan and Budapest in 1956, or in Prague in 1968, Gdansk in 1970. (On a smaller scale events of this type include the student rebellions in Warsaw and Belgrade in 1968). These unorganized, spontaneous rebellions hardly ever directly achieve all or most of their objectives, but they are invariably an important progressive force: they scare the bureaucracy, wrest out important concessions, block some degenerative processes, and bring about important personal changes in the leadership. Unpopular, authoritarian leaders like Rakosi or Novotny, or the later Gomulka, have to be replaced by more liberal ones—Dubcek, Kadar, Gierek—who are able to handle the crisis.

In the Soviet Union such explosions have not taken place in the past and are not likely in future. Obviously, in those countries which have experienced genuine mass revolution, the bulk of the working class and the intelligentsia has so fully and deeply identified itself with the new regime that subsequent crises are never so dangerous, and the sense of alienation is never so acute, as to give rise to an open rebellion. Here latent dissatisfaction with some aspects of the system and its current policy finds various other ways to express itself. These are not so stormy, violent, and directly threatening as actual uprisings, but could be equally effective in supporting more liberal and progressive factions of the political leadership, and in producing a series of desirable social reforms. This is in fact a possible mechanism of the future democratization of the Soviet Union, holding five basic factors in play: (1) a successful domestic policy, especially of economic development coupled with (2) favourable international conditions of relatively stable peace and détente, (3) a strengthening of the internal position of a more liberal political faction, (4) at the same time progressive intellectuals create a new socialist culture which brings to collective consciousness alternative, more humane possibilities and thus contributes to (5) the formation of a powerful progressive public opinion which exerts pressure on the political leadership and irresistibly pushes it towards democratization.

It might be objected that the meeting of all these conditions is not very probable. But a cold-blooded positive scientific analysis would perhaps show that the great October Revolution had even less chance. Still it took place.

1. Emphasised by M.M.

2. Roy Medvedev, *Sowjetbürger in Opposition.* Plädoyer für eine sozialistische Demokratie, Essen 1973. (To be published in English translation by MacMillan London, late 1975.)

3. Marx, 'Kritische Randglossen zu den Artikel: "Der König von Preussen und die Social reform". Van einem Preussen, *Vorwärts*, 10 August 1844.'

4. Some instances of urgent, not yet theoretically fully elaborated needs are: participation in social decision-making, peace with social justice, creative free time, making room for individual and group initiative within global planning, a synthesis of centralism and decentralization, national security without big standing armies, national self-determination that goes together with internationalism, the closing of the gap between the developed and underdeveloped nations, the control of natural surroundings without a suicidal waste of resources etc.

Socialist Democracy

Roy Medvedev's epic history, *Let History Judge* ends on a relatively optimistic note: notwithstanding the dreadful ravages of Stalinism, 'a solid foundation was laid for a truly socialist democracy'. In *De la Démocratie Socialiste*, Medvedev discusses what he means by this and shows in the process how great are the reforms that would be needed in the existing regime in order to achieve anything even remotely approximating to it.

The reason for this, as Medvedev occasionally notes with reference to specific aspects of the regime's functioning, is that the Soviet political system, as a system, has not basically changed since Stalin's death. What his successors inherited might perhaps best be described as a regime of *tyrannical collectivism*: 'collectivism' to denote the fact that his regime was based on collective ownership; and the old-fashioned word 'tyrannical' will do as well as more modern inventions to denote the unbridled power wielded by one man, though that power was expressed through a set of Party and state institutions. Stalin's successors have turned this into a regime of *oligarchical collectivism*, in which a relatively small minority of people rather than one man exercise power through more or less the same set of Party and state institutions, and without any effective check or control from below.

This is by no means to underestimate the vast changes which have occurred since Stalin's death in the operation of the system—most obviously the elimination of mass terror and of wholesale 'liquidation' from Soviet life, which is a change indeed, and the considerable reduction in the power wielded by the apparatus of repression. In this sense, 'de-Stalinization' has a clear and specific meaning; and the changes which have occurred may well justify the application to the process of 'de-Stalinization' of the notion of 'liberalization' in a somewhat wider sense—in the sense of a 'loosening up' in the texture of Soviet life.

In another sense, however, the notion of 'de-Stalinization' has always been misleading, insofar as it has been held to include basic changes in the nature of the political system, in the direction of its 'democratization'. But 'liberalization', in this context, and 'democratization' are not synonymous terms, nor are they even necessarily inter-related; and whatever there has been of the former process in the twenty years since Stalin died, there has been very little that is significant of the latter.

The 'democratization' of the Soviet system would require not merely this or that element of reform at the edges, but a fundamental change in what has always been the central feature of the system, namely the absolute and exclusive monopoly of political power exercised by the people in command of the party and state apparatus, or more properly and to avoid confusion, of the party-and-state apparatus. That they have claimed to hold their mandate from the Soviet people and to have its interests at heart, not to speak of the cause of socialism in the world, is neither here nor there. The fact remains that 'democratization' *would* require the end of this kind of monopoly—*either* by the reform of the Communist Party in ways that would introduce into its functioning at all levels what it now so conspicuously lacks, namely a genuine measure of democracy, with the acceptance of open debate between recognized tendencies and factions, which could not only be confined within the party but would find quite naturally its echo outside; *or* it would require an even more drastic 'pluralization' of Soviet political (and intellectual) life, with the acceptance by the Communist Party of competition with other political groupings, and the existence of institutions and organizations that would not be under its control.

In *Let History Judge*, Medvedev, while noting the 'negative tendencies' that result from the 'prolonged existence' of a one-party system, nevertheless suggests categorically that 'of course in the Soviet Union today a change to any sort of multiparty system is not possible or feasible'. But this very fact, he also adds, 'reinforces the needs to create specific safeguards against arbitrary rule and bureaucratic distortions, safeguards built into the structure and working methods of the ruling Party itself'. In *De la Démocratie Socialiste,* on the other hand, the question of one party or more is treated much more tentatively. Medvedev notes that the attempt in 1968 in Czechoslovakia to reconstitute a social-democratic party was denounced in the Soviet press and in part of the Czech press as 'anti-socialist' and 'counter-revolutionary'. But this approach to the question, he suggests, is unrealistic and fails to take into account the difficulties and complexities involved in the building of socialism (p. 132). 'One should not,' he wryly notes, 'over-estimate the social and political monolithism of present-day Soviet society' (ibid., p. 132). Different political tendencies and currents do exist and could form the basis of new political groupings, organizations and even parties.

What Medvedev is doing here, however circumspectly, is to attack the most sacred of all Soviet cows, namely the 'leading role' (i.e. the political monopoly) exercised by the Communist Party over all aspects of Soviet life. 'We believe', he writes, 'that a certain political "pluralism" would be normal, given the situation in our country' (ibid., p. 135). By this, he does not necessarily mean the coming into being of new political parties, but the acceptance, at the very least, of the existence of organizations in which the Communist Party would *not* play the 'leading role'; and he also advocates the publication of newspapers and journals run by representatives of different currents ('I would even say by non-communists') (ibid., p. 228). Similarly, his programme for the 'democratization' of Soviet life involves a clear demarcation between different elements of the structure of power, based on the belief that 'the continued exercise of legislative and executive power by one organ engenders the hypertrophy of the executive power and transforms the representative organisms into mere appendages of the executive ones' (ibid., p. 176). He recognizes that this runs counter to Lenin's own perspectives on the matter (themselves based on Marx's reading of the experience of the Paris Commune), but is persuaded by Soviet experience of the need for the kind of separation of which he speaks.[1]

The 'democratization' which Medvedev wants is not confined

to the functioning of the political system and to the liberation of intellectual activity: it reaches out to every area of life, including the process of production. He wants Soviet trade unions to play a much stronger role ('the role of the trade unions in enterprises remains insignificant, the more so as bureaucracy continues to dominate the trade union apparatus') (ibid., p. 298): he advocates more workers' 'participation'; and he favours experiments to determine the possibility of creating workers' councils, presumably to take charge of production, 'even if only in a few enterprises' (ibid., p. 299). But what he has to say on these crucial matters is perfunctory and banal: after all, *everybody* is now in favour of greater workers' involvement in the productive process, including the Soviet leaders, one of whom, and he no less than Prime Minister Kosygin, Medvedev quotes to this effect. But the question, it is fair to say, does not appear to be central to his preoccupations.

'Socialist democracy', as it may be taken to have been understood by Lenin (at least by the Lenin of *The State and Revolution*) entails in the economic as well as in all other realms of life a degree of self-government which goes very far beyond anything envisaged by Medvedev in *De la Démocratie Socialiste*. What his proposals and perspectives amount to is the further transformation of Soviet political life into a regime which, to continue along the line of classification adopted earlier, might be described as *democratic collectivism,* the counterpart, in a society in which the means of production are under collective ownership, to bourgeois democracy in a society where these means are predominantly under private ownership and control. 'Socialist democracy', on this view, would represent a much more advanced social and political system, of which history so far offers no example and of which there is unlikely to be an example for some time to come.

To speak of Medvedev's proposals as amounting to democratic collectivism rather than to the Marxist concept of socialist democracy is in no way to denigrate or belittle these proposals. What was said earlier about the positive nature of the change from tyrannical to oligarchical collectivism applies here with even greater, indeed with very much greater, force; the achieve-

ment of something like democratic collectivism, with the new
political and civic life this would inject into every area of Soviet
society, would in the given context represent an enormous advance on the present—and an advance too in due course on
capitalist democracy.

There have always been critics of the USSR on the left for
whom nothing less than a total upheaval would do, with a
workers' revolution establishing a dictatorship of the proletariat
based on a resuscitated Soviet system and accompanied by a
clear beginning of the withering away of the state. To those
possessed of such a vision, Medvedev's perspectives must appear
intolerably reformist, gradualist and so on—and they do in fact
have these characteristics. For that matter, Medvedev himself
explicitly repudiates that current of thought among others in
the Soviet opposition which he describes as 'anarcho-communist'
and which seeks the immediate replacement of existing state
institutions by new organs of 'popular power'.[2] The tragic irony
of his own position, however, is that the circumstances in which
he writes turn his own proposals, for all their would-be gradual-
ism and moderation, into demands for changes so far reaching
as to have distinctly 'revolutionary' overtones.

This might have been much less true if 'liberalization' and
'democratization' had already made substantial inroads into the
system. But not only does Medvedev have no illusions on this
score—on the contrary, he repeatedly suggests in *De la Démocratie Socialiste* that after an initial period of 'liberalization'
following Stalin's death (presumably the Khrushchev period) the
current has been flowing the other way—in other words that
there has been regression rather than advance; and it is quite
clear that he genuinely fears and takes as a real danger the
growth in influence and even the possible predominance of 'neo-
Stalinist' elements, of the people who are fighting 'not for the
widening but for the restriction of socialist democracy, for the
hardening of censorship and for the "bringing back into line"
of the social sciences, literature and art, for the strengthening of
bureaucratic centralism in all domains of public life' (DS, p. 71).

However, 'neo-Stalinism' is only one current in the Party, and
its predominance is not an accomplished fact but one possibility

amongst others. True, the 'bureaucratic' style pervades Soviet society: 'By the power which they have at their disposal, by their standard of living and the privileges which they enjoy those who belong to the upper layers of the state and party apparatus, of the economy and of the army, are still a long way removed from the workers at the lower and intermediate levels, and this affects their behaviour, their habits and their psychology' (DS, p. 335). But Medvedev sees most of these people as representing a 'conservative' rather than a frankly reactionary, 'neo-Stalinist' element in the political system. He rejects the thesis that they form a 'new class', though he refers to the possibility that by a slow (and still reversible) evolution, such a new class may be in the process of formation (ibid., p. 340). However, he believes that the 'bureaucrats' are much more vulnerable than is often suggested, and so is their susceptibility to pressure from below. What is needed is for the pressure to be applied; and he hopes that the tendency of which he is a declared member, that of the 'Party democrats'[3], will in the coming years help to supply that pressure and even turn it into a mass movement. In any case, even though this tendency has until now remained practically unrepresented in the higher circles of the Party, it is not, he suggests, without a fair measure of support in various sections of the party and governmental apparatus (ibid., p. 81).

To a large extent, Medvedev's qualified optimism is based on the fact that the dynamic of Soviet economic development is revolutionizing the productive process, and therewith the producers themselves. Thus he writes that 'by the end of the 20th century, there will certainly no longer be in the Soviet Union either peasants or workers or employees or intellectuals in the old meaning of these terms. The population of our country will be made up of highly educated and cultivated workers, whose activity will be both manual and intellectual, and who will participate in industrial production, in agricultural work, in the management of industry and in public affairs' (ibid., p. 355).

The question here is not whether Medvedev exaggerates the pace of the changes that he sees coming; nor even whether he is right about the picture he presents of its results. Much more important is his insistence—which is undoubtedly right—that the

great changes which are occurring and which will go on occurring in the productive process will have vast consequences for
Soviet society. Medvedev does not argue that these consequences
are *bound* to be in the direction of the 'democratization' of
Soviet political and civic life—only that the changes cannot but
sharpen the multitude of problems which the present 'bureaucratic' order is unable to resolve: and he is also saying that
while a hardening of the regime as a response to this is one
possibility,[4] its 'democratization' is another.

Furthermore, Medvedev believes that if radical change is to
come, it must be envisaged as coming through the reform of the
existing system rather through a revolutionary upheaval whose
nature is as vague as its prospects are remote. This is also the
view which Isaac Deutscher, writing immediately after Stalin's
death, expressed in *Russia After Stalin* and which he continued
to express in later works;[5] and Deutscher himself was only
echoing a hope which had been held in the ranks of the Opposition long before Stalin died.

It can hardly be said that the last twenty years have been particularly kind to these perspectives. But this does not mean that,
if there is to be 'democratization' at all, these perspectives of
'reform from within', of course brought about or furthered by
pressure from outside, namely from workers and others, do not
remain the most likely (or the least unrealistic) of the ways in
which it can occur. Naturally, there are people on the left who
know that these perspectives are absurd. But then, one remem-
bers that, in 1967, there were also people on the left who *knew*
that the idea of reform from within in Cechoslovakia was just
as absurd, and that wherever else it might occur, it couldn't occur
there, since Novotny and his people had the whole system under
impermeable control. Yet there *was* a Czech spring; and it took
Soviet intervention to crush the flowering of its promise. Of
course the Soviet Union is not Czechoslovakia, and there is at
present no sign whatever of the coming of a Soviet spring—
rather the reverse. Medvedev and those who, like him, want a
socialist alternative for their country are struggling against
enormously powerful and deeply-entrenched interests, forces
and traditions. They may not succeed in a relevant future. But

if or when a Soviet spring does come, there will be no 'Brezhnev doctrine' and no Soviet tanks to stop it; and the long and tortured pre-history of Soviet socialism will then at last have come to an end.

1. Even if the one-party system is maintained, Medvedev notes, representative institutions could be given vigour, particularly the Supreme Soviet of the USSR. (DS, p. 173).

2. See, e.g., his sharp criticisms of P. G. Grigorenko: 'Grigorenko proposes the immediate and total liquidation of the State apparatus whose representatives have always belonged to the class of exploiters. . . . Even though he calls himself a Marxist, his theses are those of an anarchist and have nothing to do with Marxism' (DS, p. 111). At the same time, Medvedev pays tribute to Grigorenko's 'admirable courage and honesty' and describes his internment in a psychiatric hospital as 'an arbitrary and illegal act' (ibid., p. 111).

3. Medvedev describes this tendency as 'a complex movement. It includes a large number of sub-groups with the most diverse political tendencies. Some are moderate; others propose more radical solutions and sometimes commit unnecessary excesses. As a general rule, the representatives of this current struggle both for the re-establishment and the widening of Leninist norms in the life of the Party and the State. They demand that the cult of Stalin should be completely rejected and that its painful consequences should be done away with at all levels. For them, Marxism-Leninism remains the foundation of ideology and social science, but must be adapted to the changes which have occurred in the world and to the developments in science and technology. One of the essential demands of this current is the thorough democratization of the Party and of our society in general' (ibid., p. 79).

4. 'In the future, when the conflict between diverse tendencies will extend to the leading organs of the Party, the security services may again escape from the control of the Communist Party and become again an institution independent of the Party and the State' (ibid., p. 199).

5. 'Lenin proceeded to restrict inner party democracy, and Stalin abolished it. The reverse process can begin only with the infusion of democracy in the Communist Party. Only from there can freedom of expression spread to other bodies, covering an ever wider range, until a fully fledged Soviet democracy comes into being, backed by a high industrial civilization and by an up-to-date socialist system.' (*Russia After Stalin*, London, 1953), p. 174. See also, e.g. *The Prophet Outcast*: 'On the face of it, the chances of revolution are still as slender as they were in Trotsky's days, whereas the possibilities of reform are far more real'. (p. 312). For a similar 'optimistic' view, see also Deutscher's last book, *The Unfinished Revolution* (London, 1967).

Détente and Democracy:
A view from the U.S.A.

The problems of détente and democratization appear in a different light to a revolutionary Marxist situated in the United States, the heartland of world imperialism, than to a dissident in the Soviet Union such as Roy Medvedev. Our immediate adversaries are different and so are our tasks and tactics. Moreover, while we have certain demands and aims in common, our respective programmes and perspectives are not the same.

Nonetheless, an East-West discussion of these questions is a welcome precedent provided it serves to remove mis-understandings and clarify the points of agreement and dis-agreement between us. This kind of unofficial exchange of views ought to be expanded, regardless of the vicissitudes of détente.

The Nature of Détente

To begin with, what are the essential factors of 'détente'? This is a three-sided set of accords negotiated by Washington, the mightiest capitalist power, with the leaderships in Peking and Moscow, bureaucratic representatives of the largest workers' states.

A reliable clue to the real character of these agreements can be deduced from their birth. The détente came into being at the height of US military operations in south east Asia. The Nixon-Kissinger visits were designed to enlist the aid of Peking and Moscow in the efforts of the American interventionists to check the Vietnamese revolution and fore-stall its victory in the south.

What did the different parties to this deal give and what did they get? The initiator, Washington, secured co-operation from Mao and Brezhnev in pressuring Hanoi to accept and abide by the terms of a cease-fire agreement in the civil war against Saigon. These were ratified in the Paris peace accords of January 1973 after final concessions were exacted from Hanoi under the impact of Nixon's mining of Haiphong Harbour and the Christmas terror bombing of North Vietnam. Moscow and Peking went along with them.

The North Vietnamese Communists and their allies hailed the accords as 'a great victory' but the accords were really a compromise that recognized the *de facto* military stalemate. The Vietnamese people have not yet won the national unification and self-determination they had been fighting so long and so hard for. Thieu's ugly capitalist dictatorship was kept in place. Eighteen months later the adverse aspects of the truce stand out more clearly than they did when the accords were signed. Despite the withdrawal of US ground troops 'with honour', the fighting continues unabated in the disputed zones of the country. Washington sends massive aid to bolster Thieu and holds the threat of 'reintervention' over Hanoi's head if it fails to observe the terms of the truce. Such are the first bitter fruits of détente diplomacy in its place of origin.

At the time we Trotskyists condemned the complicity of Moscow and Peking in this squeeze upon a sister workers' state and the anti-imperialist National Liberation Front. It was a flagrant betrayal of the interests of the Vietnamese people and the world revolution, another blot on the record of the Stalinist regimes.

For this reason we would take exception to Medvedev's assertion that 'the improvement of relations between the largest powers on the planet has thus proceeded not at the expense of other countries and nations; it benefits all mankind'. The Vietnamese have already paid a heavy price for détente. They are the first but will not be the last to do so.

Another sequel to the accords with their secret clauses has been the formation of a third coalition government in Laos where the balance of forces is even more favourable to the revolutionary side.

Main Elements of the Deal

The détente is a momentous turning point in post-war world politics, especially in Washington's policy. It represents a pronounced tactical shift by the strategists of US imperialism in their ways and means of policing the precincts of world capitalism and maintaining their international hegemony. From the end of the Second World War, Washington's cold warriors worked to halt further advances of the anticapitalist colonial struggles by any means necessary, to contain and isolate the Soviet bloc and China, and even spoke of 'rolling back' the workers' states.

A combination of factors have forced the political and military executives of the US ruling class to alter their course. The most favourable precondition for détente was the persistence and deepening of the Sino-Soviet rift that had already undercut the possibility for common action in support of the Vietnamese. It enabled the American statesmen to play one capital against the other, extracting advantages for themselves from each other while undermining both. How ironic that the White House has assumed the posture of being good friends of the bureaucrats in both Moscow and Peking!

However, the openings offered by the Sino-Soviet split were coupled with some serious reverses suffered by the almighty capitalist rulers. The heroic resistance of the Vietnamese prevented the Pentagon from smashing their liberation struggle by purely military methods. The mounting antiwar protests that drove Johnson from office threatened social stability at home. The worsening international economic situation impelled Washington to take emergency measures to counter the increased competition for markets from its main capitalist rivals. These circumstances led the US policymakers to cut their losses in Vietnam, withdraw their troops and reduce bombing, and rely more on the Soviet Union and China to pressure Hanoi. Kissinger praised the Russians before the Senate Foreign Relations Committee on 19 September 1974 for helping the United States 'extricate' itself from Vietnam.

Nixon and Kissinger held out substantial inducements to both capitals. The Kremlin was anxious for closer diplomatic arrangements through periodic summit parleys. For internal and external reasons Brezhnev is as committed as Khruschev to the improvement of relations with Washington and his fortunes hinge to no small degree upon its success.

The huge grain purchases at a low price enabled the Soviet bureaucracy, as Medvedev points out, to overcome temporary food shortages and fend off domestic discontent. Moscow awaits larger down-payments in its quest for 'peaceful co-existence'. It wants access to American technology, scientific know-how, and credits for long-term capital projects involving billions of dollars. It seeks passage of a trade-bill awarding favoured nation status.

Peking for its part promptly received trade concessions from the United States, membership in the United Nations, the opening of diplomatic relations, support to its ally Pakistan in the conflict with India, and the wind-up of the farce of treating Chiang Kai-Shek's Taiwan retreat as the legitimate government of China.

Has Détente Assured Peace?

Nixon, Mao, and Brezhnev unanimously hailed détente as a great step towards world peace. The Soviet leader's trip to the United States in June 1973, as B-52s were dropping their deadly cargo on Cambodia, was acclaimed by the American Communist Party as 'a milestone on the road to a lasting peace'. The last Nixon-Brezhnev summit talk was headlined on the front page of the 5 July 1974 *Daily World,* the US Communist Party paper: 'Moscow Pact Greeted for Peace Assurance'. The American followers of the Kremlin are now beating the drums for an all-out campaign around this theme. The national chairman of the CP, Henry Winston, described détente as 'the main all-pervasive issue upon which the salvation of mankind depends' and all the party's activities are at present subordinated to this celebration.

The people of the world who are weary of the cold war want to believe that this is the case and that the easing of tensions among the Big Three has created a more relaxed atmosphere in international relations. If only we hadn't been regaled with the same propaganda in the days of Yalta!

The exorbitant Stalinist claims for the virtues of détente as a pledge of world peace fly in the face of some deadly facts. Détente hasn't yet brought peace to Vietnam. It hasn't achieved more than a temporary suspension of hostilities in the Mid-east. When Moscow suggested that a joint Soviet-American force be sent to Egypt during the October 1973 war, Nixon called a full-scale nuclear alert. The two superpowers came closer to the brink of nuclear confrontation than at any time since the Cuban Missile Crisis of 1962.

Détente has not tied the hands of the US militarists and monopolists in either southeast Asia or the Mideast, the focal points of conflict between the imperialists and workers' states today. Washington is ready to brandish its bombs any time the revolution threatens to upset the status quo and Peking or Moscow overstep the bounds of the spheres of influence allotted to them.

Some Previous Experiences

Over the last forty years we American Marxists have had ample occasion to test the costs and consequences of similar pacts made between the occupants of the White House and the rulers in the Kremlin. Roosevelt's recognition of the Soviet Union in 1934 after Litvinov's visit led the American CP to support him and his re-election. This popular front turn cut off the possible formation of an independent labour party by the industrial unions and disoriented the widespread mass radicalism in the United States for the rest of that decade.

The Yalta agreements arrived at by Roosevelt, Churchill and Stalin not only contemplated a division of control over Eastern Europe but actually resulted in the decapitation of the revolutionary movements and the restabilization of the shaken capitalist regimes in Western Europe (a task accomplished with the connivance of the Communist parties at the close of the Second World War).

The class-collaborationist line now being pursued by Moscow and Peking is therefore hardly a novelty in the history of Stalinism. It is the extension, the logical consequence, the implementation under current conditions of the anti-Leninist concept of 'socialism in one country' masked by the innocent designation of 'peaceful coexistence', Stalinist style.

As revolutionary Marxists, we believe that every workers' state from Havana to Hanoi, from Belgrade to Moscow, has the right to engage in diplomatic, economic, and even military arrangements with capitalist governments that protect and promote their own welfare. We tirelessly propagandized in this country against 'containment' of the Soviet Union and, from 1949 on, for Washington's recognition of the People's Republic of China and the lifting of its blockade.

Our objections arise whenever and wherever such agreements are concluded by the government of one workers' state at the expense of another, contravene the interests of the world working class, and injure the progress of the international anticapitalist cause. In a poem on détente, published with the seal of official approval in *Izvestia*, Yevtushenko wrote: 'There is no contradiction with the laws of the class struggle.' The rhapsody of the poet, exhilarated by a mixture of kvas and cola, does not harmonize with the realities of the case.

In return for economic and diplomatic concessions the conservatized rulers in both Peking and Moscow have colluded with the imperialists to maintain the status quo against further revolutionary convulsions. In the Mideast, Moscow's search for good relations with the Arab bourgeois regimes is carried on to the detriment of the revolutionary forces in that area and even to the damage of the local CP's. Peking opposed national independence for Bangladesh, aided the Ceylonese bourgeoisie in crushing the youth rebels there, backed Nimeiry, the Sudanese butcher of the Communists, and welcomed the repressive Shah of Iran. Its support for NATO and the European Economic Community shows that the needs of the class struggle in Western Europe count for nothing in its eyes.

A slackening of the nuclear arms race would benefit both the American and Soviet peoples. But it is fallacious to think that long-lasting peace can be achieved so long as imperialism endures. The disarmament negotiations that have been going on for ten years have produced negligible results. The SALT talks are stalled.

The major block to arms reduction, not to speak of total disarmament, is the Pentagon's refusal to yield the superiority America's monopolists need to maintain their world domination. The United States possesses three times as many nuclear warheads as the Soviet Union, yet its military advisers insist that this margin must not only really exist but be so perceived by all other countries to keep them in order. Meanwhile the US military budget, this year at ninety billion dollars, depletes the resources of the Soviet Union which must scrimp to keep the balance of force at present levels, even though both sides wield 'mutual assured destruction' (MAD).

This background is pertinent to the objections correctly expressed by Medvedev against the orientation of several prominent Soviet nonconformists who have looked hopefully to capitalist circles in the West and American congressmen in particular to put economic and diplomatic pressure upon the Soviet officialdom to relax its repressiveness. They apparently do not understand what Jackson and his ilk are angling for. Jackson, the Senator from Boeing, the darling of the Chiefs of Staff, and the patron of Defence Secretary Schlesinger, is no friend of human rights.

Détente is a bipartisan policy supported by the majority of Republicans and Democrats alike, all staunch upholders of the interests of imperialism. The differences among them are purely tactical and subsidiary. Jackson, for one, is not opposed to agreements with the Soviet Union. He demands only that these be 'mutually beneficial so that they can be implemented and carried out to the satisfaction of both countries'. He and Schlesinger outspokenly champion 'hard bargaining' to make sure that the Soviet 'industrial-military complex' is not strengthened to the disadvantage of the American.

These capitalist representatives have as little concern about promoting civil liberties in the Soviet Union as they have in promoting them in South Vietnam, South Korea, Spain, or

Latin America. They are primarily bent on protecting America's imperial power and profits. To further their hard bargaining they have seized upon the issue of emigration of the persecuted Soviet Jewry. This has the added benefits of catching votes and dovetails with their aim of increasing US arms aid to Israel. They demogogically pose as patrons of civil liberties in the Soviet bloc to distract attention from the even harsher treatment of dissidents in Iran, Indonesia, Brazil or Chile and, above all, to extract further concessions from Moscow. The Kremlin is disposed to liberalize Jewish emigration if the US will drop its trade discrimination.

Moreover, the devout defenders of the dollar democracy have a stake in the maintenance of Stalinized police states which they can hold up as the inevitable outcome of a proletarian revolution and a true image of socialism. This is the heaviest handicap Stalinism imposes on the socialist movement in the West.

Who Are the Dissidents' Allies?

The Soviet dissidents are embarked on a heroic and historic struggle for democratic liberties. Their goals can be fully realized only through the overturn of the bureaucracy and the inauguration of socialist democracy. They need and deserve sympathy and support from every one concerned with human rights and the cause of socialism.

We American Trotskyists, in accord with the policy of the Fourth International, have done our utmost to disseminate their demands and to show our solidarity through public protests and university teach-ins, through publication of their statements, manifestos and writings and through publicizing the plight of the victims.

Our protests on behalf of the Soviet oppositionists find no common ground with anti-Soviet elements connected with the capitalist ruling class and similar forces who exploit the existence of dissent for their own reactionary aims. The Soviet dissidents would be well advised, we believe, to adopt the same guidelines. Roy Mevedev soundly criticizes Solzhenitsyn and Sakharov for their overtures to the Western Right as an ally against bureaucratic repression. We agree with the *New Left*

Review editors that the only trustworthy external ally 'in the struggle for a genuine democratization in the USSR is the international working class and its collective organizations', especially those striving for socialism.

The Road to Socialist Democracy

The most significant fact about the Soviet oppositional movement is that, despite victimizations and capitulations, it has managed to survive and make its ideas known through various channels at home and abroad. This irrepressibility is itself a victory, a sign of the vitality and necessity of the urge for freedom. As Trotsky wrote prophetically in 1938 at the height of Stalin's terror that cost him his life: 'the laws of history are stronger than the bureaucratic apparatus' that hopes to outmanoeuvre them.

The nemesis of the bureaucratic tyrants is at work. All their persecutions, arrests, imprisonments and slanders can no longer clamp a grave-like silence upon the Soviet peoples. One way or another the voices of their authentic spokesmen will be heard.

The viewpoints of the oppositionists are politically heterogeneous and range from the far right to the extreme left, from religious reversion to Leninist revolutionism. Moreover, the 'New Left' there is as variegated, confused and fragmented as its counterparts in the West have been—and far smaller.

Roy Medvedev's reputation as a historian is as outstanding as that of Solzhenitsyn in literature and Sakharov in physics. But he occupies a different and more radical place in the spectrum of unorthodox tendencies than these other eminent figures. Unlike them, he is an avowed Marxist, a Communist who aspires to revive the programme of Leninism in the struggle for a socialist democracy.

Although expelled from CPSU in 1969, Roy Medvedev identifies with the tendency aspiring to democratize the party of the privileged bureaucratic caste from within. In his book *De La Démocratie Socialiste* this 'party democratizer' has projected a platform that proposes to block off the re-Stalinizers in the leadership, support and put pressure upon the more liberal and moderate elements in official circles to grant greater reforms more quickly, and in this way gradually introduce 'socialism with a human face'.

He envisages an alliance between the most enlightened part of the apparatus and the most active segment of the intelligentsia backed by the people. The process of democratization will be controlled from above by the CP and the government within the framework of the Soviet Constitution and the changes from the top will be induced by pressure from the party ranks and the masses. Medvedev cites Hungary and Poland as examples of a successful process of real democratization directed from above (see note, p. 386).

His programme appeals to the progressive natural and social scientists and academicians, philosophers, historians, high technical personnel and other sectors of the Soviet intelligentsia. Their yearning for greater freedom of thought and access to information and knowledge, for the unobstructed exchange of ideas and opinions at home and internationally, is evidence of the growing contradiction between the expanding material and intellectual forces of production and the governing structure of the degenerated workers' state. His ideas parallel those put forward by the intellectuals and technocrats in Czechoslovakia before 1968 who paved the way for the downfall of Novotny and the 'Prague Spring'. His reformist, legalist blueprint copies the specifications of the Dubçek tendency.

The ideas and presence of these elements alarm the die-hard bureaucrats who come down on their heads, not only because of their importance to economic development, but because of what they reflect and portend. Beneath and behind this upper layer of critical intellectuals is the ferment of dissatisfaction among the broad masses that they obliquely articulate in a premonitory fashion. 'A rising wind stirs the topmost branches first.' Their cries for democracy are a forerunner of more radical plebeian demands that can issue from the rising generation of workers and youth, a symptom of more profound psychological and ideological stirrings among the people.

It is a sad commentary that the degradation of the October revolution under Stalinism has thrown the Soviet peoples back to a civil status below that attained by the revolutionary gains of the bourgeois era. They are obliged to fight for such elementary democratic rights as freedom of expression, the right to an individual opinion, freedom of association, assembly and publication, even to exhibit abstract art. This paradox is an expression of the law of the uneven development of historical formations in transitional periods.

At the same time this ongoing struggle to restore the liberties promised by the October Revolution and inscribed in the Soviet Constitution is inseparably intertwined with directly socialist tasks in the areas of economic construction and the democratization of state power. The achievement of these combined tasks, which is still in an embryonic stage, will inexorably culminate in a showdown between the bureaucratic oligarchy and the oppressed masses.

Roy Medvedev's position and proposals should be viewed in this context and perspective, in the dynamics of the unfolding of the inescapable political revolution in the USSR. In the name of morality and justice he wants the truth to be known, falsehood to be exposed, the rights and liberties of the people to be observed and amplified. These are worthy objectives.

However, the means that he recommends are not suited to attain that end. He writes in the last chapter of his book on 'The Forms and Methods of the Struggle for Socialist Democracy in the USSR' that 'the transition from an autocratic regime to a democracy is always attended by the heightening of political struggle and the intensification of political passions' (p. 358). This observation does not augur well for his proposal that benevolent bureaucrats orchestrate and guide the process of transformation in a peaceful and gradual manner without forceful and autonomous intervention from the insurgent masses.

When that stage arrives, neither side will conform to the arbitrary stipulations and quarter-measures of the liberalisers. They never have in previous revolutionary situations. The entrenched totalitarians will fight to the death to defend the bases of their privileges and power while the workers and peasants on the offensive will hardly abide by the restrictions and edicts of the hated authorities they have risen up against. The clash of arguments will have to eventuate in a test of force.

Many of the nonconformist Russian intellectuals also look for their allies to the technocrats at home and to the liberal forces abroad. Unfortunately they pay less attention to the conditions and problems of the workers, peasants and oppressed nationalities in the Soviet Union or to the revolutionary forces in other countries. They present no specific proposals on behalf of the masses. Clearly their programme for liberalization springs from the outlook of a Soviet elite. It reflects both their hopes and their fears, their aspirations for an end to Stalinist repression and for greater freedoms and faster progress, their fears of the 'dark and unruly plebeian mob' that has haunted the Russian intelligentsia (and not them alone!) for over a century.

Their isolation from and distrust of the masses is evidenced in Medvedev's reservations on the possibility of a mass movement arising in the absence of a major crisis and bringing about thoroughgoing political changes, even though such movements have emerged—only to be misled and crushed—in Poland, Hungary, and Czechoslovakia. He is not being consistently democratic, although his demands appear very audacious in the existing Soviet climate.

The balance sheet of the antibureaucratic movements from above in the Soviet bloc since Stalin's death attests to the unrealistic and erroneous character of his expectations. The Khrushchev flush of reforms proved to be restricted, came to a quick end, and have been succeeded by a greater intolerance of dissent. Solzhenitsyn's exile provides a measure of the extent of the bureaucratic concessions; his world renown saved him from being jailed or executed, as he would have been under Stalin's rule. The continued punishments inflicted on others, loss of work, imprisonment and torment in psychiatric wards, shows their limits.

After the intervention of the Kremlin's troops and tanks, the neo-Stalinist leaders, Kadar, Husak and later Gierek who replaced the used-up Ragosi, Novotny and Gomulka, have kept a tight rein on the liberties of their peoples. Their regimes hardly provide a model of socialist democracy. In fact, this levy of reformists is held in reserve to rescue the Stalinist system in emergencies. In view of the manifest bankruptcy of bureaucratic reformism in Eastern Europe, one wonders how Medvedev holds fast to its efficacy and necessity for the USSR.

In his review of *The Gulag Archipelago*, Medvedev does not gloss over his differences with the novelist's reactionary views. Yet he writes: 'Solzhenitsyn has dealt a heavy blow to Stalinism and neo-Stalinism with this book. None of us has done more in this respect than Solzhenitsyn.'

He is subject to a similar judgment. His staunch search for the truth about Soviet history despite its deficiencies, his criticisms of the methods of the Soviet oligarchy, his campaign for democratic liberties are courageous initiatives, notwithstanding his elitist outlook, reformist programme and utopian perspective. They are a progressive ferment in Soviet life and culture today that can serve to crack the bureaucratic crust and create openings for later oppositional breakthroughs by the more decisive social forces still to be heard from.

The harder and longer he and his cothinkers can press for democratic reforms, even under a more favourable relationship of forces, the sooner the limits of their line will be disclosed and the way cleared for the next and broader phases of the anti-bureaucratic struggle for socialist democracy.

The programme and prognosis of the Fourth International for the regeneration and development of Soviet democracy is better known in the West than in the East where it has been suppressed and shamelessly distorted since the defeat of the Left Opposition in the 1920s and Stalin's Moscow Trial frame-ups. It envisages the overthrow of bureaucratic domination through the independent organization, mobilization and self-action of the rearoused workers, peasants, youth and progressive intellectuals. This revolutionary struggle against social inequality and political repression cannot be waged along with or through any reformed section of the ruling bureaucracy. The possessors of power will not surrender the sources of their material and political privileges without a fight. The road to a full-fledged socialist democracy will have to arrive at the insurrectionary action of the oppressed masses, whatever preliminary and intermediary phases the process must pass through.

Its climactic point is unlikely to come about quickly or all at once. It will have to be prepared for and worked towards by partial measures that will enhance the self-confidence and self-reliance of the oppositional forces headed by authentic representatives of the working masses. Without concealing or yielding their own positions, programme and perspectives, the Fourth Internationalists will support whatever democratic demands and forward steps are proposed and fought for by other oppositional elements and act with them for their realization. That is the basis for a united front between us within as well as outside the USSR.

Medvedev has characterized his critics among the Soviet oppositionists to his left as 'anarchists' whose provocations play into the hands of the most reactionary bureaucrats. This unjustifiable accusation has been directed by liberals of diverse persuasions against revolutionists many times before. Fighters such as Grigorenko appear to us as the most consistent Leninists and the most resolute and intransigent anti-Stalinists. They have no illusions about restricting the leadership of the democratic struggle to the regenerated officialdom that has already succeeded in derailing the antibureaucratic revolts in Eastern Europe.

Medvedev refers to 'the political passivity of [the Soviet] population' as an irrefutable reason for disregarding and discounting their potential for generating a 'mass movement capable of bringing about any real political change'. This is a short-sighted outlook on the ways and means of democratizing the Soviet Union.

It is undeniable that the international class struggle has been fundamentally conditioned throughout the postwar period by the parallel passivity of the Soviet and US working classes. The pronounced absence of these potentially most powerful social and political forces in the contemporary world has permitted the Soviet bureaucracy and the US monopolists to operate with a minimum of inhibition and to act in collusion against the development of the international revolution.

This situation has caused sincere socialists in both camps to take the prevailing state of affairs as fixed and final and they write off the revolutionary potential of these decisive sectors of the proletariat. They forget the force of the Marxist maxim that 'the emancipation of the workers must be the task of the working class itself'. When he says that action by the broad masses of the people can come 'only as a result of serious political or economic crises' and that the 'prospect of such crises seems neither probable nor desirable', Medvedev leaves out of consideration the fact that a crisis is not truly a crisis until it is recognized as such by the broad masses. Their level of political consciousness is a vital ingredient.

Has this historian forgotten how the independent action and Soviet organization of the labouring masses under the Bolsheviks was responsible for the victory of October? Apparently under the blight of Stalinism this memorable lesson has faded from the consciousness of his generation.

But there are more recent manifestations of the capacity of the proletariat to throw off its political passivity and to enter into struggle against their bureaucratic masters: Hungary in 1956, Czechoslovakia in 1968, Poland in 1970-71. In Stalin's heyday many cold-war ideologies in the West insisted that the totalitarian tyranny in the Soviet Union was so airtight that its monolithism could never be broken from within but only smashed from without. The growing dissidence to date shows how superficial and myopic this prediction was.

The same applies to the United States. During the cold war, many mistakenly held that the future would not see any serious internal opposition to the course of the American imperialists. The black liberation, student radical, and antiwar movements of the 1960s have demonstrated that discontent and dissidence among the masses can break through the strongest barriers.

The political passivity of the Soviet and American workers is not everlasting. Specific conditions created their frame of mind; new conditions, now in the making, can and will change them. Genuine socialist democracy will not be delivered from the hands of benevolent bureaucrats and certainly not from the imperialists who are the foremost enemies of democracy and socialism. It will have to be regained by the Soviet masses for themselves. That will be as glorious a day as October 1917 for the Russian people and for socialists all over the world.

23 September 1974

The need for Socialist Dialogue

I read Comrade Roy Medvedev's article[1] with great interest. The ideas which he develops in it are representative of a whole current within the soviet intelligentsia which still adheres to socialism and which is trying to make a contribution to the birth of a real socialist democracy in the USSR. Medvedev sees this development mainly in terms of 'initiatives' taken by the enlightened section of the bureaucracy—by 'our leaders', as he calls this section. He makes a distinction between leaders who are dogmatists, rightists, conservatives, even 'reactionaries', and those leaders who belong to the 'new generation'. Although he mentions the 'frustration and growing dissatisfaction which exists among the broad masses and the intelligentsia', he seems to have little belief in any effective pressure being applied 'from below'. He writes: 'the people have learnt to become so silent, and have acquired such a sense of guilt, that no individual dissenters—not even small groups of dissenters—can give rise to a mass movement capable of bringing about any real political change'. Neither does he believe (and rightly so) that pressure from the West or 'international public opinion' will be effective in clearing the way towards democratisation of the regime.

This 'west' and this 'international opinion' are not homogeneous. There is a 'west' influenced by imperialism and capitalism, and there is a 'west' represented by the workers' movement and the revolutionary movement. Having said this, I would like to make the following comments on Comrade Medvedev's article. In my opinion, he exaggerates the beneficial effects of 'international détente' on the Soviet leaders. This détente is a limited, conjunctural one, interspersed with serious crises; and above all, it is complemented by a politics of class collaboration on an international scale. Comrade Medvedev has not gone sufficiently into the question of the 'leaders' and of the divisions and antagonisms between them. This is a historical and sociological phenomenon, linked to the tendency of bureaucratic caste to crystallise as such over a much longer period than was ever foreseen. This bureaucracy is effectively divided into tendencies which express the permanent struggle within it not only over the varying economic and political interests (the interests of special advantages and of power) but also over how to hold down or reflect the pressures exercised on it by the social context and ultimately by the masses. For this is a constant pressure, however 'cut off' the 'leaders' may feel from real contact with 'their base'.

This bureaucracy, then, is very differentiated. Its 'toughest', most authoritarian and absolutist section is that which is composed of the high party bureaucracy, the army and the police. In these conditions it is an illusion to believe that the bureaucracy can 'reform itself' through its 'understanding' of what is necessary and useful for the country. It is very important to study the interbureaucratic struggle from close to, and to understand that a real revolutionary process might effectively begin with serious splits within the bureaucracy which would reflect the growing pressure from the masses; but it would be ill-advised to count on 'initiatives from above'. In my opinion, the changes which are going to come in the USSR will be the result of a complex interaction between the new human forces generated by on the one hand the economic and cultural development of the USSR, and on the other hand revolutionary victories on an international scale, particularly in the European countries (both east and west). The evolution of these two phenomena will differentiate the bureaucracy still further, weakening it and enabling the pressure of the masses to be exercised more freely and effectively. This whole process will then acquire the form of a real political revolution. To take just one example, a victory for the socialist revolution in the advanced countries of Europe and the installation of a socialism based on self-management could be the decisive historical factor which would be the catalyst in a real revolutionary process in the USSR itself.

It must be hoped that there will from now on be a permanent dialogue between the socialist-orientated democratic opposition in the USSR and the international revolutionary movement which is fighting for the project of a socialism based on self-management; this will clarify the decisive problems for the development and future of the USSR and will seal the political solidarity of both in the fight for a common aim.

15 August 1974

---

1. Which we reprinted in 'Sous le Drapeau du Socialisme', No. 62.

The Machine or the Masses?

At the end of his study 'Problems of Democratization and Détente' Medvedev says that the West would be making a mistake if it imposed on the USSR conditions precedent to economic co-operation. These conditions of democratization, liberalization and free movement of people and exchange of ideas would, he argues, then constitute an ultimatum and the right-wing forces in the Soviet Union would then use this as an excuse for isolation and the stepping up of oppression.

Could this in fact happen? What interest could push the capitalist states to demand as a condition precedent to doing trade that freedom of discussion should be included in the deal? Would the capitalist states be so deeply attached to liberties as to make themselves their defenders in all countries before even trying to sell in them their surplus commodities? In reality, these states of the West have no interest whatsoever in democratization of the authoritarian states of the East and in particular of the USSR. If its 'statist' regime were transformed into a liberal regime as regards citizens' rights, the USSR would become, for all the peoples in the world, an example, and so a danger to the capitalist powers. As things are now this is not the case. Furthermore, the establishment and development of liberties in the USSR would permit new values to appear, would stimulate the development of thought, and would give a new outlet to the development of productive forces which had become once again socialist in character. In such an outcome the capitalist powers have not the slightest interest: the socialist economy would be able to compete with, and to surpass in certain fields, the capitalist economy. The capitalist powers are accordingly very much in favour of the existence, in the so-called socialist countries, of police states

which throttle every attempt to undertake research except that
determined by some 'genius for life' appointed by the Party,
which reduces ideology to the explanation of the past 'after
the event', without offering any perspective for the future.
Medvedev is certainly wrong in fearing that the capitalist
powers might impose such an ultimatum as a precondition.
The best service that the Russian regime has rendered to the
capitalist powers was precisely creating and maintaining, under
the red flag of socialism, a police state. Medvedev seems to
have lost sight of this basic fact.

He reproaches Sakharov for having asked the American
Congress to vote for the Jackson Amendment—which proposes to refuse the most favoured nation clause to the USSR
if she does not accept as a precedent condition the free circu-
lation of ideas and of people. He says that if the Congress
adopted the Jackson Amendment, economic sanctions which
would follow against the USSR would do harm to those who
in Moscow are proposing to democratize the new Constitution.
This argument seems to me to be opportunistic in character.
In fact, the American Congress will understand its own interest
very well: namely, to do nothing to cause the democratization
of the USSR. But Medvedev, who is opposed to economic
sanctions when they are proposed by Sakharov, develops a few
pages later on a contrary argument. When dealing with the
shortage of cereals in the USSR in 1972, he makes the sup-
position that if the Western capitalists had refused to sell
wheat to the USSR, the Russian masses, because of their discontent, would have been able to obtain political concessions.
After having said elsewhere several times that nothing is to be
expected from the masses, 'from down below', here he is
saying that if the masses were hungry, their dissatisfaction
would compel those in power to make concessions as regards
liberties! It is hard to imagine any power refusing liberties to
well-nourished masses and surrendering powers to them when
they are starving! Moreover, history reminds us that the
starving do not ask for liberty but for bread. So one may
suppose that a refusal on the part of the West to make de-
liveries of wheat would not help action for democratization

in the USSR but would, on the contrary, allow the conservative forces to turn their country still more inwards on its own resources: and would thus have had the same consequences which Medvedev feared from the Jackson Amendment. So, Medvedev, at one point an opponent and at another a defender of economic sanctions, does not explain this contradiction in his position.

There is another contradiction in his study: he supposes that if the 'rightist Shelest' has been removed from the leadership of the Communist Party of the Soviet Union, this is not by reason of the nationalist mistakes of which he has been accused in the Ukraine, but because Shelest (and also Voronov it seems) opposed Nixon's visit to Moscow. Medvedev cites the dismissal of these 'rightists' to stress the point that there are struggles between different tendencies in the leadership of the Communist Party of the Soviet Union. Some comments on this point would seem to be called for. In the first place, the characterizations given to the various individuals have only a very relative meaning: if a man who opposes the visit to Moscow of the most cunning representative of American Imperialists, is a 'rightist', how should those who welcome him with open arms be characterized? Subsequent events (the Pinochet-Kissinger armed coup in Chile and the Watergate affair) in a certain sense justify Shelest's position, do they not? But that is not the contradiction that can be held against Medvedev. Could one say because he was in disagreement with the rest of the leadership on a question of general orientation, that a militant was thrown out? Can one take delight in the measures that are taken against this person (albeit a rightist) who was in disagreement on a particular point, and at the same time ask that everyone should have the right not always to be in agreement? Is freedom also a matter of expediency, to be given to Sakharov and refused to Shelest? In reality, is it not precisely because it is possible for some people to get rid of the 'rightists' Shelest and Voronov without any explanation being given to the workers, that it is also possible to paralyse Sakharov, to banish Solzhenitsyn and to condemn Kuznetsov to death because he once had the intention of clearing out!

Another confusion appears in relation to the interests of the left in capitalist countries. This new confusion seems to me due to the fact that Medvedev tends to identify 'left' and 'pro-Soviet'. Once this identification has been made, every deficiency of the USSR in democracy and in civil liberty will be harmful to the left in the capitalist countries. To be sure, propaganda from Moscow has long created the impression in the minds of all Soviet citizens that the only true left in the capitalist countries is that which belongs to the Communist Parties, the other so-called left forces in these countries being only reactionary and disguised fascist formations. But Medvedev might well dissociate himself from this hackneyed misconception. In the Western countries there is a left that has no attachment to Moscow, a left that cannot be attacked for what takes place in the courts of Leningrad or Prague. Because of the existence of this left, which does not pay homage to Moscow, the officially pro-Soviet left (that is to say the Western Communist Parties) no longer chalks up against its account everything that happens in Moscow, everything that happens in the authoritarian countries: its propagandists now are content to argue primarily by making comparisons with the past, by saying certainly that everything in the East is not perfect but that there has certainly been progress. Can one then believe that the revelation of crimes committed by the various powers who have successively usurped the revolution of October 1917 can paralyse the development of the forces of the left in the capitalist West? It is naive to believe that the forces of the left in the West are going to turn to the Kremlin to say: 'You are upsetting us, be nice, free Kuznetsov, bring back Solzhenitsyn, rehabilitate Grigorenko and we will win votes when it comes to the elections'.

The leaders in Moscow have other things to do besides making difficulties for the left in the West. If they do sometimes concern themselves with them, it is solely in order to make things worse for them: they have no interest whatsoever in governments of the left establishing themselves in Western Europe. They like, when they have to engage in discussions, to have before them direct representatives, officials of capitalism, of the factories and of the banks. The development of economic exchanges between the USSR and its satellites on the one side and the Western states on the other is on the following terms: the Soviets will always gain by dealing with the real bosses. They will gain in rapidity of execution, in guarantees for the future and in the ease with which business is done. That is why they will always prefer Giscard to Mitterand, and Heath to Wilson. So it doesn't seem to me that it will be as a result of pressure from the left in the West on Soviet power that one should expect a liberalisation of the Russian regime.

By the same token it is not possible to follow Medvedev's ideas when he fears the use that the right might make of revelations that could be made about lack of freedom in the USSR. This argument has sheltered all the criminals who have committed murder in the name of socialism. In the Western communist parties it has sheltered all those leaders who have denied all their members the least right of criticism. ('You are serving reaction, comrade, you speak like the enemies of the Party' . . . and expulsion soon then follows!) If the right can say that the Soviet regime is the complete opposite of democracy, that is because it is true. Medvedev reproaches some of the opposition with having got things out of proportion in comparing the USSR to the regime in Southern Africa. This reproach is not justified. It dodges the important question of the relationship between what a regime says it is and what it actually is. In South Africa, apartheid is officially racist, segregationist, no one hides the fact, and many whites boast about it. In Germany before 1945 the regime was officially Nazi, fascist, no one disguised it, the extermination of the Jews and of Communists was there in the published programme approved by practically all those good people. These regimes did not try to disguise the quality of the goods sold. Pinochet-Kissinger deceive no one. Their military fascist and pro-American regime does what it says. The Soviet regime on the other hand does the exact opposite of what it says. It calls itself socialist and witholds liberties. It calls itself workers' power and it takes away the jobs of workers who criticize it.

It calls itself peasant power and it has brought production of wheat to a level below that of 1914! It is in this sense that we heap abuse on it: it has made use of the hopes that it gave birth to in the world so that it might commit murder the more undisturbedly. The Russian opposition that compares it to apartheid in South Africa seems to us to fall short of the truth.

The whole argument developed by Medvedev rests on the following fact: in the USSR the working class and the peasantry are politically passive, whilst in the state apparatus and the Party, at the lower levels particularly, some reasonable people understand the necessity for change in the internal policy of the country. This is not the time nor the place to go into the history and the causes of the political demobilisation of the Russian workers. The descendants of the workers in the Putilov Works are not their heirs . . . Dispossessed of their rights and of all their powers, the Councils of Workers, Peasants and Soldiers are not now even an historic memory . . . but the political passivity of the workers and the peasants is not only a consequence of the death of democracy in the USSR. It is also one of its causes. For all its lack of democratic development, the system has continued to exist these 55 years. Economic growth will go on as long as consumption of goods shall remain the raison d'etre for all progress. Medvedev has shown this: even with an incompetent leadership, growth will go on thanks to the extent of the natural resources. Material aspirations will continue to dominate social life. Cultural aspirations can only gain a niche after material provision has been made for them. Has Medvedev in fact provided an explanation?

If it is a fact that there are factional struggles in the leadership of the Communist Party of the Soviet Union, that the external and internal policy of this leadership is the result of constant compromises between rival tendencies, it is necessary to find out on what bases these tendencies are built: are the bases economic? Nationalist? Historical or related to different generations? Are they ideological? What are the different social strata of which these tendencies are the expression?

Schematically, one would tend to believe that the Right in the Communist Party of the Soviet Union would be the political representation of the Stalinist apparatus that is still there and of the hundreds of thousands of accomplices and informers who helped put millions of innocent people into the labour camps. But would this simplistic explanation still hold water when Medvedev speaks of 'the increased weight of the Right'? If its influence is increasing, where has the new blood come from on which the old Right has been able to feed? Have we yet again to wait for some groups of small party and state functionaries to become conscious of cultural needs and constitute a new social stratum aspiring towards liberty and winning itself political representation in the leadership of the Party? We might have to wait a long time for that; the politico-police apparatus will get the better of these aspirations of the lower cadres by giving them more important responsibilities. From then on appetite for power, even though very rudimentary in form, will replace all desire for social liberalisation. Was not this the road of all those honest revolutionary workers whom their Party succeeded in transforming into policemen without scruples?

So is there no way out? Are the hopes of our Comrade Medvedev illusory? Is the courageous struggle waged by those in the USSR who want to rehabilitate socialism, then without all hope?

Behind the shield that the Western Communist Parties have provided for them, the Stalinists and their successors have committed their horrific crimes. It is the certificate of socialist authenticity which the Western Communists delivered to the USSR which has allowed these crimes to take place. So action seems in the first instance to lead in the direction of members and electoral supporters of the Western Communist Parties so as to demystify in their minds the character of the Soviet State. The Soviet leaders regularly make display of their meetings with the Secretaries of those Communist Parties which do homage to them. The point of these meetings is to give proof to millions of oppressed Soviet citizens that their leaders are the leaders of socialism in the world and that they command the confidence of all those who are exploited. This is the sole purpose of these meetings. So, to bring it about that the Communist leaders in the West should no longer be able to claim either to represent all the Left or to speak in the name of all the workers, to help develop in Europe a new socialist left that is neither anti-Soviet nor pro-Soviet, is indeed to work for the conditions for bringing about a democratic modification of the Russian regime. But is a modification sufficient?

Comrade Medvedev does not develop his line of thinking when he writes that exchange of men and ideas calls for the development of Marxism. He sees this development coming from a modification of methods of ideological work, a more flexible propaganda, the renunciation of archaic and dogmatic formulae. He calls also for a sincere scientific analysis of international events and revolutionary experiences in the twentieth century. This last point is more fundamental than the others.

The nature of the Soviet state, the nature of the relations between the party and the state, the nature of the relations between the masses and the party ought to be thoroughly studied. Already Trotskyist comrades have dealt with these questions. They have done so from the point of view of defending their theory. Their studies took as their point of departure the thesis that Trotsky presented to the 4th Congress of the Communist International in 1922. But at that time was not the ill already deeper than Trotsky could guess? Those who make history cannot describe it because they do not see it. Was not the state which Lenin and Trotsky laboriously tried to build already ineluctably a totalitarian state?

In 1904 Lenin published *What is to Be Done?* He set out his conception of a centralized disciplined party giving all power to a directing centre, including that of appointing and dismissing members of all the subordinate leaderships. In *Iskra* (of which Lenin was one of the editors) the organ of the Russian Workers Social Democratic Party, and at the same time in *Neue Zeit*, the review of the German Social Democrats, Rosa Luxemburg published straight away a criticism of Lenin's theses, under the title 'Questions About the Organization of the Social Democratic Movement in Russia'. (This criticism is better known under the title 'Centralism and Democracy'). She there studies aspects of what she calls 'the barracks spirit of ultra-centralism advocated by Lenin'. Not only does she reproach Lenin with inappropriately generalising to all the socialist forces of Europe the particular conditions in which the bourgeois intellectuals in Russia came to socialism, but she shows that: 'It is precisely rigorous despotic centralism which characterises opportunist intellectuals'. She rejects the organizational propositions that Lenin put forward: 'Nothing would more certainly enslave the working class movement, still so young, to an intellectual elite thirsty for power, as this bureaucratic armour in which it is immobilised so as to be turned into an automaton manoeuvred by a committee'.

In this context she advocates, against opportunism and personal ambitions, 'the autonomous revolutionary activity of the proletariat'. At the same time, Rosa Luxemburg published in *Neue Zeit* her article 'Mistaken Hopes', which studies the relationships between the mass and its leaders: 'The masses' own intelligence in relation to tasks and the means of fulfilling them is an historically indispensable condition for socialist action, just as the unawareness of the mass was in past times the condition for the actions of the dominant classes . . . Such is and such will remain the dominant tendency of the socialist movement: the abolition of 'leaders' and of a mass that is 'lead' . . . the abolition of this historical foundation of all class domination'.

We can consider that the secret dismissal of this or that leader, the laying off of this or that militant, Sakharov's gradual procession to the stake, the treating of Grigorenko as a lunatic, the condemnation of Kuznetsov, so many other heinous crimes as yet unknown but already done, are only the most tragic aspects of the domination of a narrow class over an unaware mass.

Leninist centralism and its barracks-like spirit: are they not the causes of the lack of democracy in the USSR? For, in the last analysis, the capitalist encirclement, then the world war, then the cold war, then détente, then peaceful coexistence, then development of economic exchanges: none of these events has brought democracy to the USSR, neither under Lenin nor under Stalin, nor under Malenkov, nor under Bulganin, nor under Kruschev, nor yet under Brezhnev.

The new socialist Left in Europe which needs to be built up would do well to set itself this problem: 'How can we help restore to the Russian proletariat its autonomous revolutionary activity?'

The Socialist Opposition in Eastern Europe and the Western European Left

A whole series of questions arise in connection with the appraisal of 'the Prague Spring of 1968'.

Was such an attempt at a new democratic socialist alternative bound to fail, or was its failure the outcome of errors in the 'new course'? If so, what were they? Were the aims too radical, or is the contrary nearer the truth: that is to say, did it seek to compromise with conservative forces within the country and above all with their international centre, the leadership of the Communist Party of the Soviet Union?

Does the military intervention of August 1968 and the 'normalization' which followed mean the end of such attempts in Czechoslovakia and Eastern Europe, or is this only the beginning of an inevitable historical process?

In what ways can the socialist countries of Eastern Europe develop after the defeat of the Prague Spring?

In this process, what is the present and likely future role of the socialist opposition in Czechoslovakia and of the oppositional currents and groupings in other Eastern European countries?

How does this opposition interact with the struggle of the 'left' within capitalist countries, and what relations should the left in the West establish with this opposition?

The overthrow of the Chilean Popular Unity administration in 1973 gave a new dimension to the Czechoslovakian events of 1968: in a world divided into spheres of influence by the two super powers is any real attempt to change the system possible?

What position should those revolutionary forces which are trying to change the political status quo adopt towards the policies of détente between the blocs?

Let us try to briefly answer these questions in the light of the experience of the six years which have elapsed since the beginning of the Prague Spring.

First, one should resolutely oppose the thesis according to which this attempt to rehabilitate socialism was inevitably doomed to failure in advance. To accept any such view would amount to admitting that existing socialism is the one and only genuine form of socialism, and that any attempt to change it must end up either in a counter-revolution involving a return to capitalism, or in intervention by the Soviet Union. On the contrary, The Prague Spring did not give evidence of any crisis of Socialism as a social system, but it did reveal a crisis in the Stalinist form of Socialism, when this is applied to a country as developed in its political and economic levels as Czechoslovakia. From such a viewpoint the attempt to rehabilitate socialism in Czechoslovakia in 1968 had *specific features*. It is certainly no accident that precisely in this country the crisis reached such a depth, nor that, on the other hand, it found such auspicious conditions producing social forces mature enough to overcome it in a positive way. But at the same time this crisis had *common, basic features* which it shared with the evolution of other countries on which the Soviet pattern of socialist statehood had been forcibly imposed. That is why the crisis itself, and the new course which it generated to resolve itself, could not be limited to Czechoslovakia and were, of necessity, reflected in the total evolution of Eastern Europe.

It would certainly be useless and superfluous to stress the fact that the aim of the Prague Spring absolutely precluded any return to capitalist society, but assumed the reinforcement of socialism and the opening of new prospects for its future evolution. In this sense the Prague Spring was not a new fact. It is only necessary to recall Khrushchev's attempt, after the XXth Congress of the Communist Party of the Soviet Union, or the Polish 'October', or the overthrow of Rakosi in Hungary in

1956, to say nothing of the specific course followed by Yugoslavia as a result of the conflict with the Cominform in 1948.

Up to now all these attempts have been characterized by the fact that they have involved partial reforms of existing institutions—changes which did not touch the basic principles of the Stalinist pattern of socialism, namely the Communist Party's monopoly of power, the State ownership of the means of production, the absolute control of the flow of information, censorship, the conception that State organs, trade unions and other organizations are simply 'transmission belts for the Party's decisions', and the subjection of State sovereignty to the 'class interests of the socialist camp', which is to say to those of the Soviet Union. The Prague Spring involved a more flexible application of the leading role of the party, greater efficiency in the economy, greater independence of the mass organizations, an easing of repressive and administrative methods, the recognition of errors as expressions of the 'personality cult' unrelated to the system itself, more egalitarian relations with the USSR, and so on. One could say that it represented a certain *liberalization* of the system, carried through from above by the leadership of the party, which itself determined the time when the 'people' were mature enough for the reforms and how far they should be carried. The masses, or the 'rank and file', were not invited to intervene in this process; they were only its object. The initiative was intended to remain in the hands of the leadership, which would thus retain the freedom to cancel its concessions at any time.

After January 1968 it seemed that in Czechoslovakia too the question was to carry out such a liberalization 'from above'. But given the *existence of a Progressive opposition* within the party, the discussion on the extent of these changes and the limits of the movement was carried over from the leading organs of the party to the public at large. The masses then began to ask questions about the why and wherefore of these changes, and they wanted to know the intentions of the leadership. Later on, they formulated their own specific demands and their own proposals. In other words, they insisted on becoming the 'subject' of politics. In spite of spontaneous support for the Dubcek leadership, both Communists and people outside the party demanded institutional transformations, reforms of the system which would guarantee that past errors could not be repeated, that the executive would be effectively controlled by the public and that the citizen's democratic rights would be firmly rooted within the system. It was not so much liberalization, in Czechoslovakia in 1968, as *democratization of the system,* a democratization which could not be limited to a few piece-meal changes but had also to extend to the root principles of the Stalinist system.

The mistake of the Dubcek leadership lay in the fact that it vacillated a long time between 'liberalization' and 'democratization' and that when the whole evolution—principally under the pressure of the popular masses—was already unambiguously headed in the direction of democratization, this leadership was not able to draw the necessary consequences from it at the proper time.

These were, namely:

a. to draw up a clear-cut programme of changes and their limits (the Programme of Action had already become out-dated at the time of its adoption in practice by the movement);

b. to speedily remove discredited people from leading positions, especially by convening the extraordinary congress of the party as quickly as possible;

c. at the same time, to limit the development of extremist states of mind and all tendencies to seek reprisals for past errors and crimes;

d. to permit discrimination within the party between the progressive and conservative wings while guaranteeing freedom of expression for both;

e. to be aware of the distrust of our movement and even more, of the opposition to it from conservative forces within the Soviet leadership and the leaderships of the Warsaw Pact countries, and to face them: on the one hand, by assuring them that the alliance commitments would be respected on our part, while on the other warning that any attempt at interfering in our domestic evolution would, if necessary, be by military and popular action;

f. to seek out allies in the commonwealth of socialist countries (Yugoslavia, Rumania, China) and in the international communist and socialist movements (as well as among the currents of the 'new left' in the West) and to try to arouse the sympathetic understanding of the countries of the Third World.

In analyzing these mistakes, we find an interesting similarity between the position of Dubcek and that of Allende: the former believed in the fairness of the Soviet leadership and the conservatives in his own country; the latter believed in the fairness of the army and of the opposition; both thought they could beat their opponents by 'tricks' and manoeuvring; both were unable to mobilise the masses at the proper time, even though they were already prepared for the utmost sacrifices.

In order not to be misunderstood, let me say that I do not mean that Czechoslovakia should have defended itself militarily at the time of the invasion. By then it was already too late. Mobilising the army and the popular masses and telling the Soviet leadership, with the utmost clarity, that we would not draw back, would have been the only solution in order to *prevent* invasion. Had this been done, it is likely that the Soviet leadership would have carefully weighed its decision to intervene militarily, since this would have involved incomparably more catastrophic consequences. It would probably have decided instead in favour of some form of economic pressure (which might have been just as effective); it would have relied upon the conservative opposition within Czechoslovakia and it would have sought to make use of its political influence in order to impose a compromise which might have seriously limited the future evolution of the Prague Spring but which would not have stopped it altogether.

The defeat of the Prague Spring has certainly been a serious blow to the movement for the revival of socialism not only in Czechoslovakia, but in the other socialist countries as well. It has brought reinforcement to the dogmatic conservative forces.

But 'normalization' has by no means eliminated the causes of the crisis, and that is why the tensions, the contradictions and the need to look for new solutions are continuing. This view is supported by the upheaval of the Polish workers in 1969-70 and the subsequent downfall of Gomulka, by the economic reforms in Hungary, by the public stand taken by Soviet 'dissenters', by the deepening of the Sino-Soviet disagreements, and similar developments. After economic levelling out and equalisation of the differences between socialist countries resulting from their integration within the Comecon framework, differences between these countries have been gradually erased. What now stand out are common features, including crisis phenomena.

In these conditions economic development, the need for modern technology, scientific achievement, specialist and international contacts in Eastern European countries and in the USSR come into more and more striking contradiction with the rigid centralist bureaucratic structures of the system and thereby make felt the need for transformations and reforms. This is true within the circles which hold power, and it is still more so among the public. The defeat of the Prague Spring undoubtedly delays this response, and makes it more difficult to build an opposition within the Establishment especially in Czechoslovakia, but it cannot stop this process of change. The left forces must prepare for the *next period of transformations, reforms and upheavals; not excluding spontaneous outbursts in the Eastern European countries, the USSR included.*

In politics one cannot prophesy firmly but one may assess the likely future evolution by starting from an analysis of the present condition of affairs, the tendencies within it, the relationship of forces it contains. In the same way that we reject that type of fatalism which claims that every attempt to change anything is doomed to failure, we must also condemn other species of fatalism in which changes are inevitable, and which therefore concludes that the present crisis will automatically end up in a transformation. Objective conditions and the need for change do unquestionably exist. But what is crucial is to know whether one will find the forces capable of understanding them and making use of them in order to secure change. We must also take into consideration the fact that the present system in the USSR possesses enough reserves to be able to carry on for a long time yet avoiding any catastrophic crisis.

In the USSR there is an *alliance of a part of the summit of the hierarchy with the technocrats and the managers and with the military elite*. This grouping is awake to the ideological vacuum which has developed since the denunciation of Stalin's crimes, and it tries to staunch it partly with a new Russian nationalism, and partly with the ideal of a consumers' society which would best satisfy the material wants of the citizen (see *The New Social Contract* by A. J. Liehm). It is also aware that it cannot succeed as autarchy, and that it needs the economic cooperation of the advanced capitalist countries. That is why it pursues a policy of decreasing tension and seeks to make contact with the West. But it is afraid of any relaxation whatever on the domestic scene, because it wants to keep absolute control of power and does not want to offer any ground for mass initiative. True, such a policy can result in obtaining some social support and in deferring the necessity for deep-going changes, but none the less it cannot prevent the birth of new conflicts and new tensions (especially those between the USSR and the countries she dominates, as well as between the nations within the USSR; to say nothing of those between the diverse social groups of Soviet society as a whole, within which differentiations are increasing). In such conditions the USSR, together with the other countries of Eastern Europe, could grow to become developed countries of a nationalist, militant and authoritarian type which will then have very little in common with the image of a socialist society.

But under certain conditions, the existing contradictions and tensions may become so acute that they may, unexpectedly and quite suddenly, give rise to spontaneous outbreaks of discontent. These outbreaks will necessarily turn against the holders of power: the party bureaucracy and the police: and they could even take on an anti-socialist form, or degenerate into a settling of accounts. In some cases they may end with the downfall of the political leaders (as in Poland in 1969-70), while in others they may culminate in failure, leading to intensifications of repression and a strengthening of the status quo. They cannot result in fundamental changes unless an alliance is forged between the workers and the progressive intelligentsia, which formulate an alternative political programme: and unless there is a political force able to provide organisation and effective leadership to such an outbreak.

It is possible, and still more likely, that *given conditions of peaceful coexistence and cooperation with the West*, the alliance of a part of the State apparatus with the technocrats and the 'military lobby' (the hierarchy of the army and of the arms industry) will lead to *technocratic reforms and, along with them, a certain amount of controlled liberalisation of political life.* The leading group will without any doubt be willing to head and superintend such a process and it will attempt to eliminate beforehand any independent initiative by the masses. But even such a limited process of liberalization will reach a point at which it can no longer be reversed; for if any economic reform is to be capable of bringing forth concrete results the political system must be reformed. This will generate a situation pregnant with a new Prague Spring in a different form and under new conditions.

It might equally well be supposed, as was the case at the beginning of the Prague Spring, that the initiative for change will stem from a part of the party hierarchy and that it will be crucial in the beginning whether these changes prevail or not. But it would be incorrect to limit the role of the driving force for these changes to components of the party Establishment. Moreover, it has already been shown that the opposition 'within the party' could find scope for its activity only because the discontent of large masses ('the potential opposition outside the party') demanded changes and new solutions. It is precisely the alliance of the opposition forces from within the party leadership with the rank and file which allowed the Prague Spring to outgrow the liberalisation framework and transform itself into an authentically popular movement having as a goal the democratization of the social system.

It follows therefrom that one of the basic conditions for a positive development in the USSR and in the Eastern European countries is, in addition to the 'enlightened opposition' within the party hierarchy, the existence of a socialist opposition outside the party and outside the official institutions of the system.

Discussion on opposition in socialist countries has ceased being theoretical and has entered into a new stage. This is shown by the creation in 1970 in Czechoslovakia of a socialist movement of Czechoslovakian citizens as a broad gathering of oppositionist forces from the left with a programmatic platform, 'the Manifesto of 28 October' and the formation of still other groupings (see *Ici Prague,* published by Editions du Seuil). It is also seen in the expulsion from the Party of a group of Hungarian sociologists (Hegedus and his friends) and in the trial of Harazsti in Budapest, as well as in the public stance taken by Bierman and Havemann in the German Democratic Republic, in the Marxist philosophers' struggle around the *Praxis* review in Yugoslavia and, especially, in the activities of Soviet 'dissenters' (Bukovsky, Grigorenko, Yakimovitch, Litvinov, Amalric, Medvedev and recently above all Sakharov and Solzhenitsyn). One cannot yet speak of a political opposition with a clear-cut programme and organizational structure, but one can see its embryo in the process of formation. Even though compact groups and dissenters are as individuals numerically in the minority, they can lean on a broad mass basis formed by the 'contesting majority' of the population in these countries. The force of these groups and individuals lies in the fact that they openly express the feelings and the yearnings of whole social layers, even of the popular majority.

For the time being, it is only in Czechoslovakia that the opposition has been crystallising a programme, together with concrete forms of activity resulting from the extraordinary situation engendered there after 20 August 1968 which involved the expulsion of some half a million Communists from the party; the drawing into activity of broad layers of the population; the existence of programmatic documents from the Prague Spring; the forging of links going back to the clandestine XIVth Congress of the Communist Party of Czechoslovakia; the existence of a group of leaders who, both in 1968 and afterwards won for themselves considerable moral authority; and the linking of the struggle against 'normalization' with broad national interests. This explains why suppression in Czechoslovakia is harshest and heaviest.

But in the other Eastern European countries as well, not excluding the USSR, the groups in power must also take into account public opinion and the oppositional groupings which are being created. These groupings publicly present their position and their alternative policies on general or specific questions. The widening of international connections strengthens their opposition and at the same time protects them from the most brutal forms of suppression.

For the most part this opposition is socialist in character, even though purely liberal, nationalistic and anti-socialist tendencies are also appearing. Their aim is not to restore the bourgeois order but to reform and transform the existing bureaucratic-centralist type of State into an authentically socialist State guaranteeing broad liberties to its citizens.

In spite of the diversity of conditions in each country and the range of opinions about specific questions, it is above all the following common demands and aims which constitute the common political platform of the socialist opposition:

1. To bring about in reality a true joint ownership of the basic means of production as a popular form of property (of the State, of a collectivity, of a co-operative, all forms implying a direct participation of working men in the direction of the economy and the distribution of the 'surplus value'), leaving a private sector in the field of trade and services.

2. To create a pluralist political system on the basis of collective ownership of the means of production allowing for participation in political life of parties other than the Communist Party. Such parties would base themselves on a socialist platform, and represent the diverse interests of different social groups with the understanding that the position of the parties with respect to the Communist Party would be one of partnership and collaboration and not one of subordination to the monopoly of a single party.

3. To develop, within such a framework, a socialist democracy which would give the citizens more rights, liberties and influence than either the system of parliamentary democracy or that of Stalinist bureaucracy. To combine representative democracy (the selection of citizens' representatives by secret poll at every level) with direct democracy (control of power through workers' councils and other forms of self-management of regions, localities, and citizens).

4. To guarantee freedom of speech, of association, and of access to information as basic conditions for the development of democratic life and active involvement of the workers.

5. To guarantee the autonomy of trade unions in defence of workers' interests which can, even in a socialist society, conflict with the interests of State power. Similar needs to be given to other mass organisations so that they can share in the exercise and control of popular power.

6. To secure the independence of the courts and control over the police.

7. To resolve the national question in a new way so that either the independence of nations, or their coexistence within a single State, will be secured on the basis of true equality.

It is significant that in the Opposition's documents the relations of production and the position of the working class in the productive process are not questioned, although the relations have remained practically the same as those of the capitalist era. It is due to the work of some Marxist theoreticians in the West that attention has been drawn to these problems in connection with the Chinese Cultural Revolution. On the other hand, the Western left often under-estimates the demand for freedom of expression and considers it as specific to intellectuals. Political change and revival of political life cannot be realised in the USSR or Eastern Europe without the development of freedom of expression and meeting even though this may only be achieved by stages.

Similarly, criticism by Western Marxists according to which socialists in Eastern European countries lack a 'clearcut programme' and 'worked-out tactics' shows they do not understand the real situation in those countries. Democratic political life calls for basic conditions which do not for the time being exist. That is why one must reckon that even in the future the movement for a revival of socialism in the USSR and the Eastern European countries will still preserve for a long time a character rather of protest, of isolated demonstrations, of spontaneous outbreaks and of a mingling of contradictory opinions. Only in the course of such a process will it be possible to clear up differences, to work out homogeneous programmes and to determine tactics. Oppositional groups and individuals are also important at present, because they make it possible to become aware of problems, of the need for differentiation and thus prepare an arena for future developments.

In addition to the political programme, another serious problem for the opposition would be finding for themselves appropriate and effective forms of activity. To the need for organized activity would correspond the form of a political party. The need to differentiate an authentically communist policy from the one practised by the Communist Party and to found a new communist or revolutionary party of a Leninist type would follow directly from this. But until now experience has shown that such a party is incapable of resisting police persecution for long and that it might also give the population the impression that the whole issue is a conflict about power within the communist movement. That is why another way appears much more realistic, the one begun in Czechoslovakia: a broad movement with a common ideological goal, formulated by the leading group and popularised in leaflets and papers of the 'Samizdat' type. Such a movement might be made up of groups and even though they had different opinions and maintained their independence in working for such aims using their own initiative and acting in the light of the concrete.

The best worked out and most finished document that has yet come from the socialist opposition in Eastern Europe is 'The Short Programme of Action of the (Czechoslovak) Socialist

Opposition' (see *Ici Prague,* Editions du Seuil, Paris, pp. 232-250). The members of the opposition in exile are an organic part of such a movement. They are in the best position to formulate a long-term programme and to seek alliances with left-wing forces in other socialist countries and also in capitalist countries. But it is neither realistic nor suitable for the general staff of the opposition movement to be outside the country and to have it lead the struggle within the country from abroad. (The argument is analogous to that of the Russian revolutionaries before the October Revolution.) On the other hand, the socialist opposition is in great need of relations with and solidarity with opposition groups in other countries of Eastern Europe as well as with the Western left.

The socialist opposition should strive to become visible and to appear in public legally, as is technically allowed by the constitutions at present in force. Its relationships with the ruling group are different from those of an opposition in the conditions of struggle under reactionary regimes. It aims at being able to display its political activity within the Communist parties and the existing institutions, and it must also create links with the representatives of the group in power who are ready for such a dialogue.

Besides the political socialist opposition, there are in the Eastern European countries other groupings having more limited goals: to defend the existing rights of the citizen (e.g.: the Committee for Defence of Human Rights in the USSR around Sakharov), to demand the rehabilitation of the victims of repression, to defend the rights of national minorities or to seek freedom for scientific research and artistic activity. Such elements are potential allies for the socialist opposition which should seek contacts and collaboration with them.

The importance we give to the socialist opposition for the future revolution in the socialist countries must not lead us to unrealistic illusions. We are only at the beginning of such an opposition movement, at the time of its birth. And we should not forget that this opposition does not manifest itself in the centres of political decision-making but at the *periphery of power. Real changes can only be worked out when the opposi-*

*tion forces outside the party framework are allied to currents
and oppositional tendencies within the party itself and its
institutions.* That will be a lengthy and intricate process: it
will comprise structural reforms conceived and applied 'from
above' and aimed at avoiding the crises and radical changes
enforced by pressure from below.

The task of the socialist opposition will be to see to it that
reforms 'from above' do not limit themselves to small doses of
liberalism, but are made use of by the rank and file in order to
win more freedom, more political elbow room or to develop its
struggles. For example, it should see to it that outbursts of
workers' struggle do not lose impetus after a few economic
concessions and that a united front of workers, progressive
intellectuals and youth unremittingly challenge the bureaucracy
in order to seize from it socialist power.

The Western left should understand that *the socialist opposition in Eastern European countries is its natural ally in the
struggle for a socialist alternative* to capitalist society, while
ruling bureaucratic regimes are merely brakes on the development of socialism throughout the world. It suffices to recall the
price that had to be paid and must still be paid by the world
revolutionary movement for all the 'errors' and 'mistakes'
committed in the USSR and the Eastern European countries
(the exclusion of Yugoslavia from the Cominform between
1948 and 1955, the intervention in Hungary in 1956, the invasion of Czechoslovakia in 1968, the shooting of workers in
Poland in 1969-70, the attempts to excommunicate China, and
so on). Reactionary and imperialistic propaganda has not caused
a fraction as much harm to socialism. The main problem is not
that reaction could exploit such 'errors' for its own purposes,
but the very fact that they were possible and might even be
repeated.

Most of the Western Communist parties don't want to be
tarred with the same brush as Russia and East European
socialism. That is why they stress that their own roads to
socialism will be different. This is a positive fact even though
it is still not openly stated why their roads to socialism need

to be different. These parties also wish for a certain evolution towards democratization of the systems in Eastern Europe. Therefore they welcome any reforms which come 'from above' on the part of the leadership of the Communist Party of the Soviet Union as well as of the other Communist parties; for they see in it a guarantee of continuity without outbreaks and without upsets which would pose for them a serious dilemma, 'whom do we support: the leadership or the masses?'. On the other hand, they are afraid of the dissenters' protests and of the socialist opposition's actions, for the latter suddenly unveil the realities in the USSR and the Eastern European countries and destroy their illusions. So they either keep silent about the opposition or condemn it as reactionary: even though the dissenters often make use of the same slogans and the same programmes as those which are proclaimed by the Western Communist parties (self-management, freedom of speech, in-dependent trade unions, access to information, freedom of movement, independence, etc.). Only some of these Western Communist parties, such as the Communist Party of Australia, ask themselves what is the character of the present system in the USSR and the Eastern European countries. ('The present Soviet societies do not have some of the attributes of a socialist society . . . . What is essential to socialism is complete liberation—economic, social and cultural. That has not been accomplished in the USSR and is not to be found in the developmental pros-pects of the present Soviet Society. . . . A society based on socialism is the definition for sketching a theoretical analysis according to which there is indeed a socialist basis in the USSR —that is to say socialist ownership, and suppression of private exploitation in the productive relations. But such a basis is seriously distorted by a superstructure which has developed or has been imposed and in which authoritarianism is a substitute for democracy and which is very far from the vision of social-ism preferred by Marx and Lenin.'—Laurie Aarons, General Secretary of the Communist Party of Australia). Most of the Western Communist parties are now taking a more critical stand than in the past about the situation in the USSR and Eastern Europe, but they only admit criticism of this or that defect, radical criticism often being stigmatised as anti-sovietism 'which plays into the hands of the enemy'.* This is precisely how the groups in power in socialist countries rationalize the suppression of any criticism or opposition.

On the other hand, the socialist opposition in Eastern Europe should see the Western left as allies, since it is struggling for another, more democratic type of socialism. It realization could form a new pole of attraction for Eastern European nations and would make easier the struggle for democratization of the present Eastern European regimes. The illusion that this process could secure help from Western governments, is, to be sure, understandable, but it is very harmful. (Such illusions are moreover fostered by the Western left.)

The Western left's struggle for a socialist alternative and the struggle of the socialist opposition for democratization of the prevailing system are two sides of the same coin. That is why comprehension, a better reciprocal awareness, solidarity and mutual support are necessary. The Western left should see socialist opposition in the Eastern countries as a permanent and positive factor in the political structure of those countries and should defend this opposition's right to exist and to express its own alternative position, even though it may not be in full agreement with it. Similarly, the political opposition in socialist countries must first of all turn towards parties and groups of the left and, in cases where they suffer persecution, express its total solidarity with them.

Concerning the sixth question: it is unquestionable that the division of spheres of influence between the two super powers throughout the world is aimed at freezing the status quo and preventing any change which might threaten the balance of power. Among such threats are included socialist changes in capitalist as well as socialist countries. From such a viewpoint the left opposition in the East as well as in the West should take a negative attitude towards understanding between the United States and the USSR, even though it gives positive sup-

* 'It is possible to contain a rebellion of one people in a single country, but not to oppose an international alliance of forces which have learned how to pursue their struggle.' (*Political Monthly*, clandestine paper of the Socialist Movement of Czechoslovakian Citizens, February 1971.)

port to the principle of bi-lateral cooperation in economic, cultural and scientific affairs between these countries as well as between the other capitalist or socialist countries. The socialist opposition in Eastern Europe *supports those policies which aim at decreasing tension and widening cooperation between States with different social systems.* It suffices in this connection to recall the foreign policy of the Prague Spring in 1968. It is therefore sheer demagogy to accuse the opposition of playing into the hands of the supporters of 'cold war'—merely because it has the temerity to exist and struggle. Such a principled support by the opposition cannot prevent it from fighting against repression and against the distortions of socialism, as well as against the great-power policies of the present leadership of the Communist Party of the Soviet Union. It is not the critic who speaks of such anomalies who weakens economic cooperation, but rather the conformist who preserves and defends them. The left should therefore reject as groundless the thesis according to which criticism of the negative sides of the Soviet leadership's policies of those of other socialist countries is tantamount to 'weakening socialism' or even 'going to an anti-communist platform'.

It is true that the defeats of both the Prague Spring and the Popular Unity Government in Chile in 1973 were possible because they belonged in one case to the sphere of influence of Soviet Russia and in the other to that of the USA. But this is only one of the causes of these defeats. We have already drawn attention to the mistakes which made such defeats inevitable. That is why we do not believe that theory according to which, given the partition of the world between the United States and the USSR, any attempt to change the system in the West or in the East is doomed a priori, to failure, and that consequently the forces of progress and socialism are condemned to remain passive.

This means that, in practice, progressive forces should take a stand against any interpretation of 'peaceful coexistence' leading to a reinforcement of the Establishments in the West and in the East. (Note the silence observed by both, on such crucial matters as the Watergate affair or on the repression of the

Soviet dissenters). But the radicals must support a policy aimed at decreasing international tension and at collaboration, not only because it removes the danger of military officials with all their consequences, but also because control by the United States and the USSR in their respective zones of influence can thereby be lessened, and because new scope for necessary changes can thus be secured.

In the controversy between Sakharov's and Medvedev's theses as to whether 'liberalization' must be a precondition for the lowering of tensions and collaboration between Eastern and Western States or as to whether such a liberalization would only be a result of this evolution, we think that Medvedev is closer to the truth. This is verified by our experiences of the period following the XXth Congress of the Communist Party of the Soviet Union.

Roy Medvedev developed in his November 1973 thesis a view according to which the process of lowering tensions obviously does not automatically change the political climate within the USSR and lead to a greater consideration for the civil rights of citizens, as is naively imagined by some commentators in the West, but nevertheless creates *'conditions preliminary to the democratisation of Soviet society'*. Medvedev stresses that, in given conditions, when the Soviet leadership is interested in political and trade contacts and cannot see it as an 'encircle- ment from without' or as a 'danger of aggression', the weight of world public opinion and even domestic opinion is increased and the leadership has to give it greater consideration. As opposed to Sakharov, Medvedev does not think that it is within the powers of Western governments to obtain certain changes by external pressure. Quite to the contrary, he thinks such pres- sures may stir up counter-pressures by conservative forces. He expects much more from the influence of Western public opinion, especially from its progressive part, from its left wing, from political parties, trade unions, students, intellectuals.

The socialist opposition in Czechoslovakia has repeatedly expressed in its documents a similar view, which is, moreover, borne out by past experience. And the fact that at the beginning of this period of the lowering of tensions, the repression in

Czechoslovakia, in the USSR and other countries has been intensified does not change the principle. The repression only reflects the fears of dogmatic, conservative forces as to the consequences of such a process. *The Policies which aim at lowering tensions and at international cooperation create new possibilities for the activities of the socialist opposition.* But these remain *possibilities* and an *arena for action*: the actual outcome of the struggle for *democratization depends on how the socialist opposition will exploit such possibilities within their countries, for democratization can only result from a political struggle by indigenous forces within the socialist countries.*

An important conclusion has to be drawn by the left: *support for policies aimed at lowering tensions and increasing international collaboration does not mean keeping silent about repression and abstaining from criticism of 'distortions' in the socialist countries.* Quite the opposite: to develop criticism of negative aspects, to protest against the repression of the opposition, to widen the arena for alternative socialist action—this is the true meaning of such policies. To accept the political status quo as unalterable given fact, leads to the loss of any prospects of socialism in the West as well as in the East.

To summarise: the Prague Spring was an attempt to solve the crisis of Soviet-style socialism by developing a new socialist alternative. Its defeat was a consequence partly of the partition of the world between the two super-powers and partly of the mistakes and lack of maturity of the movement for a revivification of socialism. But this is not the end. It is, on the contrary, the beginning of a historical process of crises, of outbursts and of fundamental changes within the power as well as within the masses, and the two currents will sometimes continue, sometimes conflict. The socialist opposition will have an increasingly greater role to play. It does not fight to overthrow the system, but to democratize it. It is an ally of the Western left in the fight for true socialism and against the political status quo. That is why cooperation and solidarity between these two forces is a primordial condition for socialist transformations in the world.

Some practical proposals:
1. To develop a serious and objective scientific discussion on

the substance and character of socialist society and to analyze, accordingly, the present state of the system in the USSR and the Eastern European countries. (In periodicals and books from publishing houses open to influence as well as in the existing institutions of the left.)

2. To study the possibilities of creating a Marxist international centre or a research institute on socialism which would be able to coordinate the efforts pursued by already existing institutes, groups and periodicals and develop its own research by taking initiatives. A preliminary condition for such an activity would be joint work by scientific Marxists in the West and in the East (including those who by their belonging to the opposition and their critical stance, have no right to lecture, to work scientifically and to publish in their own countries). It would thereby be possible to bind together theoretical research and practical experience and knowledge.

3. To ensure that scientific Marxists, sociologists, political scientists, historians, economists, philosophers, and others who are discriminated against in the socialist countries are invited to lecture, to participate in the activities of existing scientific institutes, are linked both to the left and also to academic institutions. The socialist movement would thus acquire considerable information and experience which would otherwise be lost, destroyed by repression, as well as a better reciprocal understanding and cooperation between the left world forces in the West and those in the East.

4. To organise seminars and discussions on the USSR and other socialist countries with the participation of representatives of the left from the West as well as from the East.

5. To coordinate forms of solidarity and protest against suppression of socialist opposition and dissenters in Eastern Europe (activities by solidarity committees, widening them to all the components of the left, with the possibility to create a committee of coordination at the European level, organization of joint actions, etc). To link such actions to solidarity with progressive oppositions in Chile, in Greece, in Spain, in Portugal and in other countries.

Détente and Dissent

Roy Medvedev's measured appraisals provoke in my mind reflections upon two moments in my own political experience.

The first moment is that of the crisis of the Second World War: the years 1942-45. Soviet intellectuals are now examining the evidence of these years, and are uncovering a record of diplomatic miscalculation, destructive terror, and military and administrative mismanagement whose consequences were appalling. Medvedev himself, in his discussion of *Gulag Archipelago*, focuses attention on Stalin's personal reponsibilities: his 'criminal miscalculations, his inability to prepare either the army or the country for war, his ludicrously foolish orders at the outbreak of hostilities, his desertion of his post in the first week of war, and his prior destruction of experienced commanders and commissars . . .' all of which resulted in the loss or capture of some 4,000,000 troops.

Some Western socialist intellectuals have tended to focus attention less on the military conduct of the war than upon the diplomatic bargaining at Yalta and at Potsdam which determined the balance of power at its conclusion: the trading of spheres of influence, which resulted in the division of Europe which endures to this day, and which entailed, on the one hand, the imposition by Soviet arms of a military and bureaucratic 'socialism' upon the peoples of Eastern European countries, and, on the other, of the consignment of certain Western European countries to a United States sphere of influence (whose consequences, in Greece and in Spain, can be seen to this day).

Both these lines of enquiry seem to me to be important. But there is a sense in which, for a man of my generation, neither of them falls at the exact centre of the experience of those years. For the experience was—as one lived it—that 'the war' was *'won'*, and that it might very well have been lost. It is true that as Solzhenitsyn, Medvedev and others show, it was 'won' at a cost immensely and tragically higher than might have been necessary. And it is true also, as many younger Western socialists and Trotskyists insist, that in the moment of 'winning' the war many of the democratic and socialist objectives of the popular victors were betrayed by their own leaders.

But neither of these reservations cancel out the historical event: that the Allied armies and not the armed power of Fascism emerged in control of Europe. The generations who did not live through those years perhaps assume this outcome too easily. If the outcome had been the opposite, they would now be making very different kinds of assumption. For if Franco, in the more exposed and precarious circumstances of Spain, has been able to survive to this day, I can see no overwhelming reason why Nazism and Fascism should not have endured over the whole of Europe into the 1970s: at the best one might have hoped for inner nationalist fractures resulting in terrible internicine conflicts between rival élites; at the worst a Euro-Nazism, armed with nuclear weapons, might have submerged the entire world in imperialist wars. In any case, those of us who survived in the 1970s would not be discussing these matters, since we would have access neither to any printing-press nor to sources of objective scholarship.

So that a 'victory', even if at tragic cost and partially-betrayed, remains different from that kind of defeat. And since no Western writer with the genius of Solzhenitsyn has ever composed a *Gulag Archipelago* which takes into a single view the repression in this century of intellectuals, Jews, trade unionists, socialists, liberals, communists, and ordinary people of all persuasions in Western and Southern Europe, it follows that the matter is not as vividly present in the imagination of those under 40 years of age as it remains to those of us who are over 40.

It may follow also that there is a certain difference at a deep, almost sub-conscious level—a level of experiential assumption—in attitudes towards the Soviet Union. Put in the simplest way: I cannot in the end rid myself of some kind of very deep affirmative feeling towards 'the Soviet Union', as the country whose valour saved all of us from a future of Euro-Nazism. If the Western Allied forces and the resistance movements contributed something to this outcome—and perhaps contributed rather more than Russian school-children are now told in their lessons on 'The Great Patriotic War'—none of us can doubt that the Soviet people bore the greatest part. So that all of us now living, including those who were not yet born at the time of the battle of Stalingrad, live by virtue of a transfusion from that Soviet blood.

At any rate, between 1942 and 1944 it appeared very simple when one looked at a map. Nazism possessed absolute control over an area and resources larger than the present European Common Market: every unrestrained political and administrative means was employed to fashion a military machine of formidable efficiency and power. While the Allied forces engaged in peripheral campaigns or in lengthy preparations for the opening of a 'Second Front' in Europe (content, in fact, to see 'Germany' and 'Russia' bleed each other white) the markers on the map moved to the edge of Leningrad and of Moscow and deeply towards the Urals. Then they began to move back, in a way in which, from the time of the assumption of power by Mussolini, Hitler and Franco, they had never moved back in Europe before. They moved back with astonishing rapidity, as this hitherto invincible political and military machine met, for the first time, its match; and whole armies were encircled and engulfed. Even the simplest Allied soldier, listening to the news in South Italy or on the South Coast of England, knew the meaning of these gigantic German reverses. They offered expectation of ultimate victory: an enhanced chance of survival for himself or his family: a war which might not (as one had come to suppose) endure for decades but which might reach a more proximate termination.

For the Soviet people this achievement may have taken place *despite* Stalin and Stalinism, although this was not so easy to see from the West at that time. And the resilience of the people may have stemmed from patriotic rather than communist resources. But however this is seen, some residue of affirmative

feeling towards something called loosely 'the Soviet Union'
must always remain in my experience. Even when confronted
by *Gulag Archipelago*—perhaps at such times most of all—one
thinks of the Soviet people as a people with extraordinary, in-
exhaustible reserves; with an irrational resilience; a people who,
when by every logic they are defeated, are capable of moving
the markers back across the map once again. For some of us,
in those years, admiration was indiscriminate and self-betraying;
and we can now see clearly Stalinism as the enemy of Soviet
and Western revolutionaries alike. We can also see Soviet
'dissidents' in all their variety—Solzhenitsyn, Sakharov or
Medvedev—as emblems of this astonishing resilience; driven
back into the Urals of Soviet culture, they have decided, when
defeat had seemed inevitable, to give not an inch more of
ground; they are hemmed in in their own Stalingrad. Will we
see, once again, those liberating markers moving back across
the map? This is what Medvedev asks. I have tried to explain
why this question calls up in some of us an ancient sense of
solidarity.

*   *   *

The other moment in my own political experience which
Medvedev provokes me to reflect upon lies in the years 1956-
61. In the aftermath of the 20th Congress Western Communist
Parties were thrown into turbulence, with major secessions of
'revisionists' and 'dissidents'. In Britain some of the seceders
(the *New Reasoner* group) formed an alliance with younger
socialist elements which gave rise to the 'New Left'. These
events coincided with the influential presence of the Campaign
for Nuclear Disarmament: in itself an induction of a new
political generation into affirmative action.

The Campaign advocated the immediate, unilateral renunciation by Britain of the manufacture or possession of nuclear
weapons. By some—indeed by all—this was seen, in part, as
'a moral gesture'; an initiative towards general disarmament and
détente. But opinions were divided as to the political and diplomatic context of this policy. Some supporters of CND advocated the open or tacit continuation of Britain within the
strategies of NATO. This would have entailed a continuing

dependence, in the last resort, upon a United States 'nuclear shield' which, in the view of some of us, deprived unilateral nuclear disarmament of either moral or political credibility. We in the New Left advocated the policies of CND *plus* 'positive neutralism': that is, a policy which entailed also British renunciation of NATO and the adoption of mediating, neutralist policies aligned to those of Yugoslavia, India and the emergent Third World.

It was a critical part of our advocacy that we argued that with each effective movement of détente there would follow a relaxation in military and bureaucratic pressures within both the United States and the Soviet Union. Thus the relaxation of Cold War tensions was a precondition for further de-Stalinisation, and a precondition for resuming socialist and democratic advances, East or West. I was myself especially associated with this advocacy; and since recent events—and Medvedev's own questions—have thrown this whole perspective into doubt, I should perhaps convict myself out of my own mouth.

Thus I wrote in *Universities and Left Review* (No. 4, Summer 1958):

'. . . with each month that the Cold War continues, a terrible distorting force is exercised upon every field of life. As it drags on the half-frozen antagonists become more sluggish in their reactions. Political and economic life is constricted, militarism and reaction are infused with new blood, reaction and the subordination of the individual to the state are intensified, and the crooked ceremonies of destructive power permeate our cultural and intellectual life.'

The relaxation of the Cold War would create conditions 'in which healthy popular initiatives will multiply' and (in the words of the Programme of the Yugoslav Communists in the same year) 'shatter the basis upon which bureaucracy thrives and assist the more rapid and less painful development of the socialist countries'. If the British Labour Movement were to adopt the policies of unilateral disarmament plus active neutrality (outside of NATO) this would contribute simultaneously to the acceleration of processes of democratization in the East and to the resumption of socialist progress in the West. The same perspective was still presented in the British *May Day Manifesto* (1968).

As Medvedev shows, we have been witnessing in 1973-4 an altogether different process. Summit agreements between United States and Soviet leaders, accompanied by some regularization of relations and limitation of Cold War tensions, have intensified pressures upon Soviet 'dissent' and have been accompanied by the increasing discipline of intellectual and cultural life throughout the Communist world. Does this mean that our original argument was wrong, and was based upon a merely sentimental and wishful appraisal of realities?

Such a conclusion would be premature. It is mistaken to be too impatient in our expectations. There are inner contradictions to be expected within any wider social or political process. The logic which we proposed—that relaxation of Cold War tensions provides a precondition for socialist democratization—has, although in a very general and uneven way, been seen at work between 1954 and 1974: and notably in the evolution of Eastern Europe. But insofar as democratization threatens ruling bureaucracies and also the military-diplomatic controls of the Soviet Union, we have seen a zig-zag movement with very severe setbacks—notably in Czechoslovakia, 1968.

In the Soviet Union the contradictions are especially acute. On the one hand, the repressive institutions and the repressive ideology of pseudo-Marxism have found, for decades, their major source of justification in the function of the ruling bureaucracy (and of its organs of police and of intellectual control) in defending the Soviet people from the threat of attack, from without or from within. It therefore follows that if Nixon and Kissinger can be seen driving through the streets of Moscow—and if the threat from Western imperialism can no longer be seen as immediate—then the function of the bureaucracy is itself called in question, and its repressive ideology loses further credibility. Hence 'détente' is simultaneously a moment of enhanced danger to all those whose privileged and unrepresentative positions rests upon the invocation of this function. Hence the post-Stalinist bureaucracy finds that its legitimacy is called in question, not because our earlier argument was wrong, but because it was right. If the threat from the West appears to diminish, then the old functions can only be sustained by emphasising the threat from China. (But this also involves tormented readjustments of ideological orthodoxy, and of expectations as to from which quarter to expect 'the main enemy' within).

Thus what we are now witnessing is a limited and calculated agreement, a détente based upon the regulation of great power interests from above. Both parties to the agreement wish to keep this détente firmly within control and to prevent the unleashing of popular initiatives. But insofar as *any* détente strips the reigning Soviet bureaucracy of its prime function and legitimation, this is sensed as a moment of acute danger. Controls over the life of the Soviet people are tightened at exactly this moment, to prevent that uncontrolled and self-generating liberation of (in the first place) intellectual and cultural forces which would, in the end, call in question this bureaucracy itself.

*   *   *

If this analysis is correct, then it also suggests to us certain lines of action which European socialists should take. What we are observing in the Soviet Union at the moment need not indicate a genuine and profound reversal of the tendencies towards democratization but a temporary arrest to a process which, at any time, may be resumed. Since so much depends upon contingencies—as well as upon the jockeying for power of different interest-groups within the Soviet leadership itself—it would be foolish to attempt any prediction as to whether this arrest will prove to be long or short. What has to be challenged is the complacency of those Western socialists and liberals who assume that they are only spectators in this auditorium, and that the outcome will be determined solely by events in the Soviet Union or in Eastern Europe. So long as Western social-democracy remains confined (whether by active ideological complicity or by effective impotence) within the strategies of NATO and of a 'Europe' which excludes not only Moscow but also Prague, Belgrade and Warsaw, it is itself contributing to the outcome which it deplores. It is very easy for the Western intellectual to applaud those Soviet intellectuals who have the courage to challenge their own statist orthodoxy. But since Western intellectuals, for all their vaunted (and valued) freedoms, have been unable to detach decisively one single Western society from the military and diplomatic definitions of the Cold War era, the applause has an empty sound to it.

There have of course been gestures towards such a detachment: in French truculence towards NATO, in Brandt's *ostpolitik*, and (at the level of annual conference decisions) in the professed policies of the British Labour Party. Gestures and professions are better than nothing; and they indicate that, with greater resolution, actions may ensue. If only one Western nation were to effect a democratic transition to a socialist society, were to detach itself decisively from NATO and from dependence on the United States, and were to initiate an active, probing, self-confident diplomacy, offering manifold exchanges in trade and in ideas with 'the East', this might serve as a significant catalyst. An initiative of this kind—supported by popular initiatives, exchanges by trade unionists and intellectuals, exchanges in education and in tourism—could not be presented by orthodox Soviet ideologists as the old kind of threat to 'subvert' the Soviet system. It might give great encouragement to the most affirmative elements in Soviet and Eastern European 'dissent'; and, by breaking down the old ideological deadlock, by which we are offered the alternatives of a statist and repressive 'communism' or of substantial democratic rights and defensive liberties within a capitalist society, it would point towards further perspectives of socialist internationalism.

It is of course true that such an initiative—if taken by France, Britain, West Germany or Italy—would entail an element of risk. Militarist elements in the Soviet leadership might take it as evidence of 'weakness' in 'the West' and seek to exploit it accordingly. Thus we are supposing that, if such an initiative were to succeed, it would meet with corresponding initiatives from progressive forces in 'the East', at least strong enough to hold their more regressive and militaristic leaders in restraint. And the risks would be greatly enhanced by the diplomatic and economic sanctions brought to bear by the United States and

NATO powers upon any defaulting member; by the consequent exposure of this defaulter to immediate economic and social crisis, accompanied by intensified internal class struggle. But the continued division of Europe and of the world entails much greater and continuing risks, which may be regulated temporarily but which can never be permanently ended by great power agreements. We can never move out of this international polarisation except through a process which, at the moment of depolarisation, entails great risk: and it is important that these risks be taken, not as a result of unforeseen accidents, but in a context of mounting popular internationalist initiatives.

This is to restate, in the context of the mid-1970s, perspectives which were argued in the late 1950s by Claude Bourdet and the French *Nouvelle Gauche*; by 'positive neutralists' within the Campaign for Nuclear Disarmament in Britain; by C. Wright Mills in the United States; and by Imre Nagy and the Yugoslav League of Communists. It is sobering to realise that, after fifteen years, the perspectives appear to many to be more, rather than less, utopian. Not many Western socialists today appear to have any confidence in the possibility of a peaceful and democratic transition to socialism; indeed, few appear to be examining what such a transition would entail and many would appear (from their actions) to consider that such a transition would be undesirable, preferring to develop the defensive institutions and the redistributive policies of the labour movement, so that they can get some milk from the capitalist cow for as long as she has milk to give. At the same time the younger Marxist Left, in all its varieties, falls back upon a rhetoric of 'revolution' which supposes a dramatic and violent transition to a socialism whose democratic features are problematic—a rhetoric which, whether one finds it distasteful or not, offers a perspective a good deal more utopian than the one I have sketched above. Finally, many dissidents in 'the East'—or many of those whose voices have been heard most clearly in recent years in the West—no longer hold to the perspectives of a regenerated socialist democracy which, to one degree or another, informed the Polish revisionists in 1956, Imre Nagy, the Yugoslav Communists of 1958, or Dubcek. One or two of them (if we are to judge by recent statements of Solzhenitsyn) might actually oppose any Western advance towards socialism, and would (like the Pentagon) see the detachment of any Western power from NATO strategies as a symptom of weakness.

Utopian or not, I think it is worth re-stating this old perspective for two reasons. First, it may serve to correct the rather self-satisfied stance of some Western liberals and socialists. For if one proposes this perspective, it can at once be seen that it might prove to be as difficult for a Western nation to resume initiatives independent of great-power polarities as it proved to be for Czechoslovakia in 1968: moreover, a comparable effort of self-emancipation by any Western nation has scarcely been attempted. While this does not in any way call in question the value of Western freedoms, it does suggest that Western intellectuals have efficiently preserved these freedoms for their own consumption by virtue of the fact that they have been ineffectual in using them to challenge the overall boundaries within which such self-expression remains 'safe'. The limits of Western tolerance have not yet been exposed to a Dubcek-type test; or, if they have, that test was made in unusual circumstances in the southern hemisphere. And when Allende pressed against those limits, neither he nor any Western freedoms survived the test.

Second, the perspective only appears utopian because it is presented in a way which proposes that an action be taken in advance of the necessary preconditions for that action. These preconditions are, exactly, an initial rebirth of socialist internationalism; a growing discourse between 'dissident' voices in both the East and the West; a discourse which, by proposing alternatives to the present polarisation of power, itself begins to create such an alternative, in a reawakened internationalist conscience, and in feasible national strategies. This is why one must attach the greatest significance to Roy Medvedev's initiatives. Honest political exchanges between Soviet or East European dissidents and Western socialists, unmediated by party officials and uninhibited by ideological imperatives, are a precondition for Eastern democratization and for Western socialist advance alike.

One might, in conclusion, offer some comments on the way in

which such exchanges may be conducted. And these remarks may be more usefully addressed to Western socialists and Marxists than to Roy Medvedev.

Medvedev's writings have met with a serious response from Western Marxists: in Britain notably from Ralph Miliband and in *New Left Review*. They have also met with some silly responses; and some of the silliest have come from little groups of intellectual *gauchistes*, who have chosen to call themselves Marxists or Leninists, and who pretend to speak for an (imagined) revolutionary proletariat. One has read (or heard) assertions that Medvedev is 'a semi-Stalinist', because he suggests that the next significant shift towards democratization may be initiated by elements within the Soviet Communist Party itself. It is suggested that Medvedev and all other known dissidents (as opposed to hypothetical, fictional ones) are privileged intellectuals concerned with enlarging the privileges of the intelligentsia. Or Soviet dissidents are blamed for not calling for a 'revolution' of the Soviet masses, and for not agitating in the factories and fields. In general, such thoughtless comments are calculated to throw suspicion on the motives of dissidents; to emphasise that they are intellectuals and therefore untrustworthy; and to limit or inhibit solidarity with them.

It is true that intellectuals in political movements often show characteristic weaknesses, impatience, instability. It would be tempting to reply to Western 'Marxist' critics of Soviet dissidents by pointing out that these same critics are themselves (in the main) intellectuals, who themselves exemplify—in their impatience and their instability—exactly these weaknesses. But this *tu quoque* is too easy a reply: the matter requires a little more thought than this.

First, those socialists who enlist themselves under the name of Marx might do well to attend more carefully to the unique role which, at different moments in European history, a radical or revolutionary intelligentsia has played. The traditions of this intelligentsia extend backwards for many centuries; they precede the formation and political identity of any proletariat; and in this sense the radical intelligentsia is, as a perceptive British

Marxist (V. G. Kiernan) once noted, 'the oldest regiment that
is still in the line'. If conventional history has often neglected
the creative, culture-formative role of the peasantry and of the
working class—and if Marxist historians have properly redress-
ed the balance in their writings—it is foolish to pass over to the
other extreme and to deny all value to the contribution of this
intelligentsia. For, if we leave aside the evident fact that much
of human arts, sciences, technologies and educational disciplines
would not have existed at all without this intelligentsia, there are
also specific contributions to the socialist and revolutionary
movement which intellectuals are uniquely equipped to make.

This is so obvious that it is painful to have to set it down. It
is obvious also that in a de-structured political community one
of the first tasks to be undertaken is the collection of information, the articulation of grievances, and, above all, the work of
communication. This work has always been the particular responsibility of intellectuals; and when we pass to the work of
international communication, unless the intellectuals, with their
particular skills and 'privileges', perform this work, it will not
be commenced at all.

We pass from the very obvious to the even more obvious.
And if one passes an inexpert eye over Russian history, over
19th-century populist and *narodnik* history and the early evolution of social revolutionary, *menshevik* and *bolshevik* movements also, this necessary role of the intelligentsia is at every
point confirmed. Moreover, one encounters the characteristic
Russian conflict—very familiar, one supposes, to Academician
Sakharov and his friends today—of the progressive, 'Western-
izing' intellectual, dedicated to opening up international communications, who is accused by conservative elements within
Russian society of being *déraciné* and alien to the true Russian
'soul'—and who, indeed, is sometimes expelled by this hostility
into a state of spiritual alienation. In this historical perspective,
the fact that political communications (both internal and external) are being established first of all by intellectuals, acting
without organization but with a profound sense (perhaps a
historic sense) of individual responsibility, ought not to cause
surprise. It would be, in similar circumstances, inevitable any-

where, and in Russia most inevitable of all. One seems to see, as the dust of the terrible battles of the last decades begins to settle, the familiar cast of Russian history arranging itself for (as one hopes) the less bloody and more promising contests of the future. The only cause for surprise is that some Western observers cannot see the familiarity, the necessity, the inevitability of this process; and that some of those who are most blind choose to go under the name of 'Marxists'.

My second point is, again, so obvious that I am ashamed that is has to be made. To accuse Soviet dissident intellectuals of self-interest because they are concerned with enlarging the privileges of the intelligentsia is to commit a serious breach of solidarity. It is an accusation which should not be made unless substantial evidence can be brought in support. It is an accusation which can result in the most harmful consequences: first, in limiting the instant expressions of solidarity from Western socialist and labour movements which our Russian comrades need and deserve: second, in suggesting to these intellectuals that they can expect support only from conservative elements in the West, and hence encouraging in a few of them a negative attitude towards the socialist movement as a whole.

The accusation is, in any case, very silly. Those Soviet intellectuals who are in search of privileges can purchase these at a small price: the price of their own integrity. To engage in exchanges with the West, to issue critical statements, to nourish internal communications between dissidents, is not the broad highway towards privilege in the Soviet Union. Moreover, certain forms of 'privilege' are essential preconditions for the due performance, in a craftsmanlike way, of the intellectual's proper work. Just as a joiner cannot make a window-frame without good tools and proper wood, a scientist cannot work without access to a modern laboratory and uninhibited exchange internationally of scientific papers: Zhores Medvedev has illustrated this very clearly. The fact that this is so is one of the affirmative contradictions in Soviet life: for technological and scientific advance demand that Soviet scientists be given workmanlike conditions, including 'freedoms' and international exchanges, and it is greatly to the credit of such scientists as

Academician Sakharov and Zhores Medvedev that—instead of being satisfied with a 'deal' with the bureaucracy by which scientists can be bought off with certain concessionary privileges limited to themselves alone—they have used this contradiction as a fulcrum from which they seek to lever the bureaucracy to grant such rights and freedoms to the intelligentsia as a whole: in the first place to the intelligentsia, in the second place to the Soviet people.

Intellectuals cannot serve the community effectively without workmanlike conditions. Such conditions may be material or technical (laboratories, skilled assistance, journals); or they may be ideal or spiritual (freedoms, uninhibited exchanges). Some (but not all) writers may require privacy and what appears to a layman to be excessive 'leisure' to prepare their work. A British historical journal with which I am associated, *Past and Present* —a journal with a long and distinguished association with the Marxist tradition—has recently protested against the conditions in which Czechoslovak historians have (since 1968) been forced to work. Professors whose work won international repute before 1968 are not (it seems) now in prison camps or in mental hospitals: one may be working as a translator, another as a school teacher, another as a taxi-driver. One does not object to this because one is offended by social egalitarianism; I myself have no objection to the 'Chinese' notion that professional workers should take a share, on equal terms, in the necessary work of society—that they may, for example, benefit greatly from the experience of working for a few months on a commune. I can think immediately of several British historians whose work is sadly impoverished by the absence of any life experience outside the university's walls. But when Czech or British or Soviet historians are working *as* historians they cannot do their work without the time, the access to uncensored libraries, the rights of publication and the communication with fellow-scholars which are the necessary conditions of such work.

It is of course possible that the question of a Soviet intelligentsia seeking to establish itself as a privileged group (whose privileges are not extended to the people as a whole) could arise. Indeed, for the loyal and time-serving intellectual bureau-

crat such material privileges exist and have long existed. And
the Soviet bureaucracy, by encouraging *ouvrieriste* manifestations and resolutions against dissident intellectuals, may succeed
temporarily in dividing society against itself and in driving the
most radical and courageous elements in the intelligentsia into
isolation. We will have to see how the matter goes: but it seems
to me that our Soviet comrades are, on the whole, resisting this
state of spiritual isolation, even when they are, at times, effectively hemmed in, denied rights of expression, and hence actually
isolated. Even Solzhenitsyn, who has expressed notions which
I find negative and unrealistic, has resisted with the full force of
his genius the attempt to type-cast him as an 'alien' or as a
man in pursuit of personal privilege.

I apologise, once again, for rehearsing points which should
require no rehearsal. I do not, in general, find that active socialists in the British working-class movement have any difficulty in
understanding that intellectuals require workmanlike conditions:
nor do they see these conditions as 'privileges' to be resented.
They may resent (as I do) the exploitation of these conditions
in order to gain exceptional material privileges: as, for example,
in the present controversy over the rewards (from fees from
private patients) of consultants in the Health Service. And they
may resent intellectuals, whose position is in some senses privileged, who fail to use their skills in the service of a wider public.
Those who most frequently adopt ferocious *ouvrieriste* postures
and who sow doubts as to the motives of Soviet dissidents are,
for the most part, intellectuals themselves; who, from the safety
of a university campus or the heights of North London, are
engaged in a charade in which rival sects are seeking to outbid
each other by the deafening intransigeance of their revolutionary
rhetoric. Nothing less than instant revolution and the procla-
mation, anew, of Soviet power will satisfy them at all; all manifestations which fall short of this (as all are bound to do) can
be denounced. Unrepresentative as such voices are, they have
contributed a little to confusions among the younger Marxist
Left, and have limited somewhat the expressions of solidarity
which (one would have supposed) should have come, in impera-
tive tones, from such quarters above all. Moreover, our Soviet

friends who are not familiar with these transitory 'revolutionary' charades of the young bourgeoisie must also find such expressions (if these reach their ears) to be confusing and disheartening. For they will observe that the Soviet bureaucracy and some elements in a self-styled Marxist Left in the West are playing exactly the same game.

This leads me to my final points as to how such exchanges might be conducted. If exchanges enlarge they will turn out to be deeply confusing; to overthrow many cherished expectations; to break down many ideological pre-suppositions. There is a sense in which the Soviet Union, after fifty years of severe intellectual repression and discipline, is a de-structured political community. Or it is, in one sense, altogether de-structured; and in another sense, it has only one, obligatory political structure, through the Soviet Communist Party. We are fortunate, in conversing with Roy Medvedev, to be conversing with a man who relates at many points to our own Western socialist traditions, and specifically to a Marxist tradition: we recognise common terms and sign-posts. But it cannot be expected that all conversation will be like this. On the one hand, from the de-structured political community we must expect that a people who have suffered from innumerable crimes which have been justified by a mandatory statist Marxist orthodoxy will show a profound distaste, not only for Stalinism, but also for all Marxist forms and terms. The Christian tradition will seem to some—as it seems to Solzhenitsyn—to have offered greater resources in defending the individual and the human conscience than any resources within Marxism. The children whose teeth have been set on edge by the sour grapes of paternal statist orthodoxy may have come to disbelieve not only its falsehoods but also its truths; they may suffer very large illusions as to the liberalism of the West, and they may be (as Solzhenitsyn seems to have been) seriously misinformed as to certain Western realities. In contrast to statist ideology the Voice of America may be mistaken for the voice of truth.

On the other hand, insofar as the only legitimate structuring of political life is through the Soviet Communist Party, we may expect to see unexpected and unpredictable things here also. Any historian knows that social contradictions and tensions have a way of working themselves out, not in neat predictable ways, but through whatever forms are available. People make use of whatever forms history has given to them to use. In a Durham pit-village in the 19th century the very conservative Methodist chapel may turn out to be the training school for a militant miners' leader; in Catholic Fascist Spain we may find important radical and libertarian elements within the Catholic Church; and so on. Since the inheritance of the Soviet Communist Party is in fact enormously richer than its official ideological forms would suggest, we can expect repeated evidence of social tensions working their way through within—or despite—these forms. The rhetoric of statist Marxism may be authoritarian and empty; but it remains, in form, a Marxist rhetoric, and there are strong libertarian elements within the Marxist tradition. To suppress those elements would involve (among other things) suppressing the collected work of Marx.

This is why it is foolish to criticize Medvedev because he has some expectations of renewed democratic changes initiated by elements within the Soviet Communist Party. But in fact I find it foolish and beside the point for any Western socialist or Marxist to spend time, at this particular stage, in criticizing Medvedev or any other dissident in any way at all. What we ought to be doing is *listening*. In the first place, and in the second place, we have to express solidarity, assist our Soviet comrades in their efforts to consolidate a position from which any dialogue becomes possible, listen carefully, learn, attempt to understand the new ideas and the new sensibility which has been growing up like tundra beneath the orthodox snows.

The particular privilege enjoyed by the Western Marxist or Leftist intelligentsia is the privilege of irresponsibility. Since our actions are largely verbal and command few real social consequences, we can say what we like in the way that we like. An error of political judgement, an ill-advised telephone call, lack of security with an address-list, will not bring down the arrest of colleagues or their dismissal from employment. Still less will it plunge a whole movement into disarray. Some

of us have got so used to this displaced, intellectualized context
of Leftist discourse that we indulge in the luxuries of mutual
denunciation at the drop of a hat. In the pursuit of a 'correct
line' which might be followed, at the very most, by a few
thousand people—and more often by a few score intellectuals
—we denounce A. because he has a wrong formulation on
Soviet State Capitalism and B. because he shows a tendency
to humanism and moralising. Well, if we want to be like that,
and if the discourse between East and West opens up further,
we shall find a great deal to denounce. It will keep us happy
for some years. There will be, for example, quite a lot of
Soviet humanism and moralising, since a nation which has had
a great many millions of people wrongfully and arbitrarily
killed or imprisoned has got something to moralise about, and
some knotty problems about morality, politics, the State and
the individual conscience, to clear up. It will seem to some
that the matter is not wholly closed by coming to the fine point
of a correct formulation.

I would suggest, however, that we do not take our Western
habits of intellectual irresponsibility into this particular discourse. We might indeed do better to learn a little from the
calm and responsible tone of Comrade Medvedev—and the
tone of one or two of the most recent statements of Academician Sakharov. Even at moments of great difficulty, Medvedev
has never lost sight of the primary duties of solidarity. Let
me illustrate this with one passage from his recent discussion
of *Gulag Archipelago*. Medvedev argues, with careful attention
to the evidence, that Solzhenitsyn has exaggerated Lenin's
responsibility for abuses of power. He concludes:

> . . . we remain convinced that the overall balance sheet of
> Lenin's activity was positive. Solzhenitsyn thinks otherwise.
> That is his right. In a socialist country, every citizen should
> be able to express his opinions and judgements on the
> activity of any political leader.

It is necessary to recall that Medvedev wrote these lines at
a time when the courageous but impetuous declarations of
Solzhenitsyn had exposed not only himself but also the Soviet
dissidents as a whole to a general outcry of official outrage,
and threats of administrative repression. Solzhenitsyn, when

he came forcibly to the West, made certain statements which many of us on the Western Left found to be hurtful, ill-informed, negative. How much more damaging such errors (if they were errors) must have seemed to those in the very exposed positions of Medvedev or Sakharov. And yet both men responded to *Gulag Archipelago* in the most open and generous manner, arguing their disagreements rationally, with courtesy, and within the context of mutual solidarity.

Thus we have to listen not only to what Soviet dissenters are saying but to the ways in which they conduct arguments between each other. They do not sniff around each others' legs for heresies, nor detect in each minor disagreement potential treason to the working class. They rely, *mirabile dictu*, upon rationality and persuasion; and even in the moment of refuting an argument they defend the right for an argument to be put. It seems to me that any helpful discourse between Soviet dissidents and Western socialists must be conducted in much the same way. For the time being we should not be impatient for it to have an outcome in any agreed opinions or agreed internationalist strategy; the open and rational discourse—and the information and mutual understanding which this will bring —will remain as a sufficient objective. And if some of those from the East who join the discourse turn out to be deeply hostile to all Marxism, and in search of pre-Marxist spiritual values, I hope the discourse will continue all the same. Indeed, when I read some self-styled Western Marxists—for example, the school of M. Althusser, which appears to continue on its way oblivious of the fact that the history of the Soviet Union raises certain 'moral' questions—I think that it would not matter all that much if Marxism was Christianized a little. Or, again, perhaps the problem is that as a State or doctrinal orthodoxy it has already been Christianized too much.

As regards the supposed failure of dissident Soviet intellectuals to agitate among the masses . . . Perhaps I may end with an historical analogy which might afford a little encouragement. When in 1792 Tom Paine published in England *Rights of Man* every official and quasi-official means was taken to suppress the man and his ideas. Paine was indicted and driven into exile. The book was burned by the public hangman. House-to-house enquiries were made as to his readers or supporters. Resolutions were passed at county meetings. In nearly every town and most villages in Britain there were public bonfires, when Paine was burned in effigy, and the populace were given drink to toast the 'Church and King'. And all this worked very well. The chauvinist and regressive impulses of the crowd (who had never had an opportunity to read Paine) were flattered. Those intellectuals and artisans who supported him were isolated in a sea of public hostility. But a year or two later? What the authorities had overlooked was that they had engaged in a superb advertising campaign. Every old woman (as one reformer noted, in an isolated country town) had heard about Tom Paine and wondered what he had really written. The ideas and the pamphlets began to circulate in the wake of an aroused national curiosity. Soon a book had become a popular movement. I could not say whether this is a relevant analogy or not. I know little about the complexities of life in the Soviet Union. But I do know that in history exiles have a way of returning as heroes; and that at night bonfires light up the surrounding countryside.

Problems of General Concern

Disagreements among the Soviet dissidents

A year ago we were still debating whether controversy among the Soviet dissidents was at all needed. Today this problem does not even arise, because the process of differentiation among them, so painful in its initial stage, has gone already too far to avoid controversy. This was quite a natural process. In 1966-68, when we witnessed the first great eruption of the democratic movement in the USSR, we were all united by the same demands: an end to the political repressions, the defence of human rights, the availability of information, an end to the discrimination against the Crimean Tartars, against the Jews, and against the Volga Germans. We were also united in our protest against the invasion by the Warsaw Pact countries of the territory of the Czechoslovak Socialist Republic, and in our criticism of the Stalinist past still persisting in many spheres of the internal policies in our country. But no opposition movement can continue for long if it bases itself exclusively on the *criticism* of an unsatisfactory state of affairs; the need for putting forward and defending some *positive* programme led, precisely, to differences of opinion and to polemics among the dissidents which we are now witnessing.

Among the many currents of the intellectual opposition in the USSR I should like to mention the three most important: the movement for democratic and humanitarian socialism (the 'liberal' Marxists); the movement for the spiritual renovation of society on the basis of religion; and all sorts of nationalistic movements. Of course, there still remain other kinds of intermediate currents and interests as, for instance, groups of Christian socialists. There are those champions of the Greek Orthodox Church who are for democratization; while there are others who would rather see Russia ruled authoritatively as before. Among nationalists there are some racist elements (who speak up, for instance, against mixed marriages). Apart from all these, still continuing the fight are such a-political groups as 'Amnesty' and the Committee of Human Rights headed by A. D. Sakharov. All these groups and trends have, of course, the right to exist. However, personally, I consider as the most important and the most promising in the Soviet conditions the movement for socialism 'with a human face'.

On the 'dialogue' of the dissidents with the ruling hierarchy

A Western journalist asked me not long ago: 'How is the dialogue between the dissidents and the rulers developing at the present time?'

It seems to me that although the dissenters are scattered and not numerous, yet the Soviet hierarchy has to pay attention to them both in the internal and even the foreign policy of the country. This shows itself in its attitude towards such problems as the rehabilitation of Stalin, the emigration of Jews, Volga Germans and some others.

However, we are very far indeed from a *dialogue* as this notion is usually understood in the West; such a dialogue simply does not exist. If a 'dialogue' with the authorities occurs, then more often than not it takes the form of *an interrogation* to which practically every one of us is subjected from time to time either as a defendant or as a witness.

Democratization and public opinion in the West

Soviet society is in need of many democratic reforms, and it is obvious that Western public opinion can provide quite important support for the movement for such reforms. At present, when as a result of administrative repression, Samizdat has shrunk considerably, it is precisely the Western media of mass communication which allow the views of various dissidents to become more clearly known to our own people. For a country like the Soviet Union, the influence of Western public opinion, including its left wing, will remain helpful; but it cannot have a decisive importance. The main, the substantial change can be achieved only by the country's internal forces. For us, it is important not only to have the support of Western public opinion but to create *Soviet public opinion* which, in truth, still does not exist or is only in the first stages of its awakening.

Cooperation between governments and democratization in the USSR

Of course, agreements between governments cannot by themselves lead directly to any political and economic reforms within the Soviet Union. Some bureaucratic methods can even be preserved by these agreements, as our propaganda gives a great deal of publicity to such successes of the administration. However, a refusal to reach such agreements and cooperation coming from our partners in the West could create an even worse situation of isolation and inadmissible pressure. This would play into the hands of the most reactionary elements in the Soviet leadership. In other words, in this respect there is no sensible alternative.

One should also consider that *in the somewhat longer run* many agreements on cooperation with other countries may become quite a weighty factor for change in the USSR, change which will depend on the extent of economic, technical and cultural development of Soviet society. Apart from this, only the establishing of a wide and solid system of cooperation and of economic inter-dependence between East and West will increase the effectiveness of the influence of Western opinion on the political atmosphere in the USSR. The Chinese Academy of Sciences can protest as long as it wishes against the persecution of scientists-dissidents in the USSR. Nobody will pay the slightest attention to this. If our attitude to the protests of American scientists is immeasurably more serious, this is due mainly to the fact that Soviet scientific establishments cooperate with the American ones on a series of important projects. And this cooperation is precisely the result of official agreements between the two governments.

On the pressure of the Soviet Union on Western countries

Economic sanctions as a method of pressure on the foreign or domestic policy of any country are, as we know, adopted as a system even by the United Nations Organization. The British

government to this day applies sanctions against Rhodesia, and
the United States against Cuba. The European Economic Community applied economic pressure on the military-dictatorial
régime in Greece. In 1973-74 the Arab countries quite effectively
used oil as a weapon against the West.

In the past the Soviet Union too resorted quite often to this
method, refusing, for instance, to trade with Spain, Portugal,
Greece, the United Arab Republic, Israel, and later on, with
Chile. In his time Khrushchev tried to exert economic pressure
on China, recalling from there all of a sudden all economic
advisers and specialists, which forced the Chinese to abandon
work on many important projects. The advantages or disadvan-
tages of economic sanctions always depend on the concrete
situation: sometimes sanctions can indeed bring about the
desired changes in the policy of a given country; but sometimes
they only harden and preserve the existing reactionary régimes.

Of course, many-sided economic cooperation between the
USSR and Western countries creates the possibility not only of
Western pressure on the Soviet Union but also of pressure by
the Soviet Union on Western countries. There is no doubt that
in certain circumstances our country will resort to the same
methods. This is quite often used as an argument against economic agreements with the USSR. I do not regard this argument
as a decisive one. After all, economic cooperation and trade are
practically always conducted on the basis of *reciprocity*. In other
words, cooperation benefits not only the Soviet but also the
Western economy. This is why one should, of course, reckon
with the possibility of Soviet pressure on the West, but this
should not, by any means, constitute a sufficient reason for
refusing to enter into economic cooperation. However, it should
be understood that even the most profitable commercial agreements between governments and private business should not
stifle a critical approach from public opinion.

The strengthened international situation of the USSR and the weakened position of the West

If in the second half of the 1960s the international situation of
the USSR was continually worsening, in the first five years of the

present decade we are witnessing a contrary phenomenon: we see a gradual strengthening of the international position of the Soviet Union and of its influence abroad. This is a result not only of changes in many aspects of Soviet foreign policy which undoubtedly has become more flexible than it used to be (the so-called peace offensive of the USSR). The fact is that Western countries have suffered in the last few years a whole series of painful failures in their relations with the 'third world', failures from which the Soviet Union was able to derive quite considerable advantages. Growing economic difficulties and internal contradictions between Western countries (for instance the conflict in Cyprus) also weaken the position of the West.

The Soviet Union was able to derive considerable advantages from the successes of the forces of the Left, which compensated by far for the Chilean defeat. However, one gets the impression that the most reactionary part of the Soviet leadership is interested in victories of Left and communist forces only in relatively small countries of the West which puts these countries into a state of economic and political dependence on the support of the Soviet bloc. This reactionary part of the Soviet leadership is not really interested in (rather it fears) victories of Left forces in the major Western countries which might become an independent centre of attraction for democratic and left-wing movements. This became particularly noticeable last year during the Presidential campaign in France.

Anyhow, the weakening position of the West, and especially of Western Europe, which has occurred in recent years, should obviously serve as an additional stimulus for a movement of unification of Western European countries into a more tightly knit European economic and political community. In the last analysis, this process of unification is, from the socialist point of view, *progressive* regardless of the present capitalist forms of such unification. This is why I do not understand the attitude of those groups on the socialist Left which adopt an isolationist and nationalist position rather than an internationalist one. Until now the proletarian movements and proletarian organizations in Western Europe have shown much less ability to unite their

144 *Roy Medvedev*

forces than have all kinds of bourgeois-monopolistic organizations and groups.

The gradual process of unification of Western democratic countries not only creates better conditions for peaceful socialist transformation (for instance, by the enlargement of the nationalized sector of the economy), but constitutes also an important barrier against the development of reactionary political tendencies in the Soviet Union.

If today the Soviet Union is, in the first instance, in need of an enlargement of democratic rights, of freedom, and a series of democratic political reforms, then the West, because of the development of the economic crisis, is in need of sensibly devised social-economic changes. Today that much is understood also by many bourgeois economists (Galbraith and others). The unification of precisely these outwardly different trends can become the foundation on which a viable and flourishing community of nations can be built on our planet.

According to the old legend, the King of Gordium in Phrygia rode up to the temple in a carriage. An oracle declared that whosoever succeeded in untying the strangely entwined knot which bound the yoke to the pole should reign over all Asia. Alexander the Great, according to the story, simply cut the knot by a stroke of his sword. Political, economic, domestic and other problems of big and small nations are now tied up into more complicated knots than the Gordian one; but nobody would now cut through the knot with the weapon of war. On the contrary, the main international problem consists in this that, under no conditions should the weapon of war be used. There is only one way: gradually, consistently, armed with patience and determination to untie one after another the knots of our contentious problems. In this the development of many-sided economic and cultural cooperation can be useful, not a return to confrontation and the cold war.

Is the Soviet leadership capable of making changes?
It is well known that the doctrine of Marxism-Leninism or of scientific communism justifies the use of force and the violation of many democratic rights only for the comparatively short

period of the immediate revolutionary transformation of bourgeois society. But once socialism is victorious—and our propaganda maintains that we have already entered the period of 'mature' socialism—full democracy and all the democratic rights of the individual must be guaranteed in a manner that should be incomparably better than this was possible under capitalism. Unfortunately, in this respect our performance still falls very far short of the requirements of our own ideological doctrine.

It is incorrect to ask, as Western correspondents in Moscow frequently do, 'How far can Soviet communism go towards liberalization in the field of human rights without violating the requirements of Marxism-Leninism?' It would be more correct to ask the question in a different way: 'how capable is the Soviet leadership of introducing democratic reforms within the framework of socialist society and of getting rid of the various elements of pseudo-socialism and pseudo-communism?'

Even within socialist circles in the West many people imagine that there is complete uniformity within the Soviet establishment both as regards the Soviet system as well as its management which is said to operate without any 'feed-back'. This view is schematic and false. Of course, the Soviet establishment is united by a mass of material and other privileges which it holds on to tenaciously. But nevertheless it is not uniform, and it would be a mistake to think that our leaders do not realize what is going on 'down below' among the working-class, the peasantry, and the intelligentsia. Their reaction to it is something else again.

Of course, because we have no free press or opposition, because political minorities are denied the right to free speech and free assembly, our country is deprived of many of the most important channels for 'feed-back' and this weakens the influence of society on the policies of the leadership. But in one form or another 'feed-back' exists in our system of government. And the leadership knows what is going on much better and more accurately than we, as ordinary Soviet citizens, do. We have no access to the official and secret information which includes an enormous amount of data which would not be considered secret in the West, beginning with the number of people killed and injured in industrial accidents and going on to the annual number of abortions performed on schoolgirls. As for the majority of shortcomings in Soviet life, including separate outbursts of mass dissatisfaction among workers in the provinces, the Soviet leadership is much better informed than the rank and file. We scientists, even though we specialize in social science, are no exception and our data about the processes going on in the country are too fragmentary and superficial.

With all their privileges the Soviet leadership is still subjected to quite a strong influence from below. By a whole variety of channels popular demands particularly in the economy penetrate to the very top, not to mention the growing tensions caused by economic competition with the capitalist countries. But all these influences from below and from abroad produce no single or uniform reaction in the leadership.

In the present leadership of the Central Committee of the CPSU there are nowadays no proponents of authoritarian government. Solzhenitsyn's worries about the rapid democratic changes demanded by Sakharov are completely groundless. One can clearly distinguish three main trends within the leadership.

The first of them is represented by a group of reactionaries, led apparently by Mikhail Suslov. They want a stiffening of internal policy. They are against any rapprochement or cooperation with their capitalist neighbours. In fact they would like to move backwards to a restoration of a slightly revamped form of Stalinism. In the ideological field typical representatives of this group are people like Trapeznikov and Yagodkin. Needless to say, a victory by this group in the inner-party struggle which has sharpened in recent months would have catastrophic consequences.

In the second group one can locate the more moderate politicians, whose main slogan over the last ten years has been 'stability'. Stability was what the Soviet establishment wanted. They were tired of the numerous changes and reforms of the Khrushchev era and were still quaking from the horrors of Stalin's terror, against which no-one was secure. It was this that guaranteed the victory of the more moderate section of our leadership, Brezhnev, Andropov, Grechko, Gromyko, Kosygin, and Podgorny, over the Suslov group and the Shelepin and

Semichastny group who were the main organizers of Khrushchev's dismissal.

It is impossible to deny that this group in the last five to six years has achieved certain successes, particularly in foreign policy but less so internally. But progress in many fields, especially the economy, was too slow and the need for changes has grown so much that the slogan 'stability' has now become a brake on our society's development. This has produced a significant strengthening of the so-called 'technocrats' within the leadership. These are the comparatively younger leaders, who want to modernize the management of the economy and science, and would like closer links with the West and a more tolerant internal policy. These people are without many of the prejudices and complexes of the older generation, and they are capable of bringing in reforms which, even if they will not change the basic face of our society, will open a wider road to progress and democracy.

There are nowadays quite a few of these people around Brezhnev, both among the leaders of the various union republics and area committees, and among the secretaries of the central committee and the ministers and their deputies. In the coming years and even months much probably depends on a possible alliance between these technocrats and the main representatives of the 'moderate' group.

Precisely because we have no democratic system of leadership, the role of individual personalities is especially great even though this perhaps does not fully agree with Marxist doctrine. Every serious historian must be aware that if in 1917 the leader of the Bolsheviks had not been Lenin but Kamenev, as it was developing before Lenin's arrival from Switzerland, then the October Revolution would not have occurred, but instead there would have been a Constituent Assembly with a strong Bolshevik faction. If after Lenin the head of our party had not been Stalin but Bukharin, then there would not have been collectivization in the Stalinist form nor the terror of the Thirties and Forties. And if after Stalin's death Beria or Malenkov had emerged at the head of the party, there would have been no Twentieth Party Congress and no Twenty-Second Party Congress, nor that mass liberation of political prisoners about which even Solzhenitsyn writes as though it were the result of a 'spiritual impulse' of Khrushchev's. So it is impossible to be indifferent about the possible changes in the Soviet leadership and think that détente will go on regardless of who becomes head of the CPSU and the USSR in the next few years.

Liberalizing emigration and the prestige of the USSR

I have often been asked recently 'How can an inter-governmental plan for emigration from the USSR be worked out which will save Moscow's face?'

First of all, I think that even if the Soviet Union's frontiers were fully open, there would be no massive emigration; the capitalist countries themselves would not allow it. Unfortunately our authorities consider that any significant emigration from the country 57 years after the revolution would be 'a loss of face'. In his time Lenin said that considerations of prestige have no importance for the Soviet state and that when it comes to prestige issues 'we are quite indifferent and ready to ridicule them' (Collected Works, 5th ed., Vol 45, page 239). This prediction however did not come true and the USSR like most other states remains highly sensitive to prestige issues. That is why the US Congress and any other Western state institution has much less influence than Western public opinion.

When he produced his famous Amendment two years ago, Senator Jackson thought he would get from the USSR certain concessions towards freer emigration. But the Senator did not know how to maintain enough political tact and reasonable flexibility, as a result of which the USSR repudiated the 1972 trade agreement, even though it was very useful for both sides. As a result it was Jackson himself who lost face, all the more so since Jewish emigration is currently running at the same rate as in 1974. Senator Jackson thought he could prove his great influence over the Soviet Union as well as his personal influence in the Senate. He forced the American and Soviet leaders to take account of his views. This was in itself a great achievement. But he then went on to make himself look like the old woman in Pushkin's story about the Fisherman and the Fish, and he ended up with a broken trough. The insulting remarks about me which Jackson made when he announced his candidacy for the Presidency (*New York Times*, 28 January 1975) only testify to his short temper and inability to learn the lesson of a political failure.

The 'new' emigration and the democratic movement in the USSR

Neither the wave of emigration from Russia before or after the Revolution, nor the so-called 'non-returners' in 1945 and 1946, in spite of their size (each wave consisted of between two and three million people) had practically any effect on the life and development of Soviet society. Even simple correspondence with relatives was impossible for decades. Russian life, Russian organizations, and the Russian émigré press abroad were completely unknown to us. Only at the end of the 1960s when Soviet samizdat trickled out abroad did we learn of certain Russian journals and newspapers where these articles were reprinted and commented on.

It is quite different now with the present wave of Russian and Jewish emigration. A significant part of this emigration consists of people who are well known in the various circles of the Soviet intelligentsia. Many of them are people well-known in the West and for that reason their opinions, statements, and arguments are listened to with attention on both sides of the Soviet frontier. Only time will tell how far the new Russian emigration uses the advantages of its position.

So far we see that with all their differences of opinion, at times very sharp, most of the new émigrés continue to live for their motherland. Undoubtedly this allows the best representatives of the new emigration to make a contribution towards the development of the democratic movement in Russia, possibly an even bigger contribution than they could make when they were here.

About the attitude of the dissidents in the Soviet Union to Solzhenitsyn

Today in all Soviet dissident circles, and indeed in the whole thinking section of the Soviet intelligentsia, people listen to Solzhenitsyn with attention and respect. *The Gulag Archi-*

pelago, obviously, arouses the greatest interest. In spite of all the shortcomings of the author's conception, it will always remain the greatest testimony to the terrible tragedy our people lived through.

If however many dissidents now have a different attitude towards Solzhenitsyn, this is not because he now lives in Switzerland but mainly because of his own political and religio-political statements. The notorious 'Letter to Soviet Leaders' which he published a year ago undoubtedly disappointed most dissidents. And many objections were called forth by his remarks in an interview in Zurich and Stockholm in November and December 1974 which only the Russian language journal *Russkaya Mysl* published in the West. And the collection of essays by Solzhenitsyn and Shafarevich, called *From Under the Heap of Rubbish** produced a decisive protest by most readers among the dissidents. I must say with sorrow that in the recently published book in Paris, *The Calf Butted the Oak,* Solzhenitsyn distorted the picture of Tvardovsky, who is dear to me and to us all, not to mention his comments about other editors of *Novy Mir.* Solzhenitsyn also writes with insulting disdain about Sakharov. Besides this Solzhenitsyn reproduces in his book many private, even intimate conversations with Tvardovsky, Sakharov and others. These conversations were never intended for publication and in many instances their contents have been distorted. Of course in the book Solzhenitsyn's artistic genius shines forth in all its brilliance. But when I read each new book or statement by Solzhenitsyn I frequently ask myself 'Is he not one of those great artistic people whose talent far surpasses his intellect?'

In the twentieth century Russia has given the world many geniuses. We have had not a few people who acted or wanted to act as prophets. But the conjunction of the powers of a genius, strength of will, and the complex of a prophet have only come together three times in the last hundred years: with Tolstoy, Lenin and Solzhenitsyn. But it is clear that the main thing for Solzhenitsyn remains his work as a writer and not his political activity. As a writer Solzhenitsyn will always be one of the very

* An alternative English title is *From Under the Boulders.*—Translator.

greatest of Russians. But as a prophet he will have far fewer followers than Tolstoy.

From Under the Heap of Rubbish

I personally cannot but welcome the rebirth of a free Russian press of various tendencies, even though it is published abroad. How regrettable, however, that the free expression of thought by authors published outside the Soviet Union is not accompanied by a deepening of thought; that the inquiry into the most important problems is conducted on such low levels that any serious debate is impossible; the lack of tolerance of differing viewpoints comes again to the fore, together with narrow-mindedness and dogmatism, which in the last analysis are analogous to a 'party line' of the worst kind though with a new content. Solzhenitsyn, for instance, writes in his first essay: 'For decades during which we were silent our thoughts straggled off in a hundred different directions, never hailing each other, and so failing to get to know each other, and so never to correct each other. The shackles which constrained our thoughts maimed all of us, leaving hardly any brains undamaged . . . and now, even when minds that are strong and brave try to stand up straight, throwing off that pile of crazy rubbish, they still bear the marks that were branded upon them, still suffer from the crookedness of those lasts on to which they were forced when immature—and owing to their intellectual isolation from one another, they cannot test their ideas against anybody else.' (*From Under the Heap of Rubbish*, p. 8, Paris 1974.)

There is a great deal of truth in this. But why is this description directed first and foremost against A. D. Sakharov, when it is precisely Solzhenitsyn himself and his co-authors who suffer from one-sidedness, from a tendentious subjectivity imprinted on their minds?

In the first essay of the volume, Solzhenitsyn, pronouncing on the 'deadly sins' allegedly committed by political democracy in recent years in the West, advocates the re-introduction in Russia of an authoritarian-theocratic regime, of the *non-party* or *party-less* (Solzhenitsyn's italics) rule of a 'spiritual elite', and adds that 'the ways and principles of creating such an elite and of its functioning can have very little in common with contemporary democracy' (p. 23). But is it not clear that such a regime will be nothing but a dictatorship, precisely a dictatorship of the least influential *party* of our society?

The authors of the essays, contained in *From Under the Heap of Rubbish*, especially Solzhenitsyn and Shafarevich, not only do not accept socialism and the socialist idea—they are full of hatred of socialism and are unscrupulous in the mode of their struggle against their opponents. The almanack *The Twentieth Century* already contained some essays criticizing the religious-ethical projects of Solzhenitsyn, Shafarevich and their co-authors. As to their socio-political and economic pronouncements, there is simply no basis for scientific debate. For example, I. Shafarevich, criticizing Marxism, devotes a great deal of attention to the fabrication according to which Marx and Engels defended . . . the common possession of wives as an important socialist idea. It may be worth mentioning that in his article on principles of communism Engels, answering the 'lamentations of the highly moral burghers about the common ownership of wives under communism' wrote: 'Community of wives is a peculiarity of bourgeois society; it is brought to its highest point of perfection by the community of women called prostitution. Prostitution is rooted in private ownership: destroy the latter and prostitution disappears. Far from inaugurating an era of the common ownership of women, a communist organization of society puts an end to such a condition of things.' (K. Marx and F. Engels, *The Communist Manifesto*, p. 336, London 1930.) In other, later writings (*The Origin of Family, Private Property, and the State*) Engels again showed how in socialist society the family would become more healthy and more stable than it had been under capitalism, and devoted quite a few pages to this. How can there be any basis for a discussion with Shafarevich!

Both Solzhenitsyn and Shafarevich are trying to maintain (without however adducing any proof) that in bourgeois countries 'from the beginnings of industrial production', capitalists do not exploit workers, but, on the contrary, the workers, as a result of successful strike action, 'are receiving an increasing part of the product which *they do not produce*'. (Underlined by

Solzhenitsyn, p. 10.) In other words, the workers exploit the engineers, the scientists, and the very capitalist-managers of the enterprises. How can there be a basis for any serious debate here!

Objecting to the socialist principle of *equality*, Shafarevich does not quote the famous words of Marx and Engels on how, after the victory of socialism 'in place of the old bourgeois society with its classes and class antagonisms, there will arise an association [of free producers] in which the free development of each will become the free development of all'. Shafarevich does quote, however, the crazy reasonings of one of the characters from Dostoyevsky's *The Possessed* about the destruction, under socialism, of all genius, all talent, about the lowering of the level of education, and so on, and so forth. How can there be any basis for a scientific discussion here!

In his preparatory work for *The Holy Family*, Marx took a number of excerpts from the writings of his opponents and his precursors in the camp of the so-called petty-bourgeois, bourgeois, and feudal socialism. Copying these excerpts from Marx's notebooks, Shafarevich names Marx himself as 'the author of these brilliant thoughts'. How can there be here any basis for polemic!

Referring to some rather controversial ideas of Freud on the death instinct which allegedly dwells in every one of us, and also quoting a song popular during the first years of the Soviet régime, 'We shall courageously fight for the power of the Soviets, and *as one shall die*', Shafarevich at last comes to his main theme: 'Life fully permeated by socialist ideals must lead to the universal result: *the dying off of the whole of humanity, its death.*' (p. 66) And further: '*To the immanent forces influencing the course of history belongs the yearning for self-destruction, the death instinct of humanity*'. And it is precisely 'socialism, which takes possession and subordinates to itself millions of people, which constitutes this movement and its ideal goal: the death of humanity.' (pp. 69-70) (Shafarevich's italics).

It makes no sense to argue against such statements and prophecies, because they are not rooted in the logic of scientific analysis but in the emotions. In his article Shafarevich maintains that socialism not only threatens the very existence of humanity, but also paralyses its most hopeful weapon, namely the mind. But we see that his own mind is already paralysed to a considerable degree not by socialism, but by his blinding hatred of this one tenet which in truly scientific form can save humanity from many dangers really threatening it.

Kontinent

In principle we can only welcome the appearance of *Kontinent*, a new journal which widens the margin of free discussion about contemporary topical problems. In any case, I have read with interest the two copies of the journal, though I do not share its ideological platform. However, on reading *Kontinent* one becomes clearly aware that the journal is addressing itself in the main not to the East but to the West, and that its principal task is to turn Western intelligentsia and youth against Marxism and socialism. It is quite clear that the aim of the founders of the new journal was to supply anti-communist and anti-Marxist western ideologues and publicists with new squads of professional writers and publicists from the USSR and Eastern Europe who as eye-witnesses, so to say at 'first hand', unmask not only certain perverted forms or 'models' of socialism, but socialism and communism in general. It was therefore perfectly natural and logical for Maximov to turn for support to the Springer concern. The claims made by Ionesco about the creation by *Kontinent* of a new Left ideology of which the West is allegedly in great need, are simply ridiculous and absurd. It was certainly not for the benefit of the Left that the new journal was founded. Its editor Vladimir Maximov not so long ago was still a close collaborator and protegé of V. Kochetov, for years the leader of the Stalinists in matters of literature.

I am convinced that the Western Left, including Marxists, have enough opportunity to reply to the challenge of *Kontinent*. A discussion would certainly help in clarifying many important points.

As far as the artistic side of *Kontinent* goes, there still remains a lot to be desired. The novel by V. Kornilov *Without Hands, Without Legs*, was written some ten years ago and is not the best of his prose works. V. Maramzin's *The Story of Ivan Petrovich's Wedding* did not seem interesting to me. N. Korzhavin's *Essay in Poetical Autobiography* has been circulating a long time in typescript in the Soviet Union, but has not proved a great success in Samizdat. The article by A. Sinyavsky *The Literary Process in Russia* is too superficial, though it contains some important reflections. The memoirs of Cardinal Midszenty, published earlier in the West, have not aroused the interest of the Soviet readers of *Kontinent*. To me the most serious article seemed to be that by L. Kolakowski *Three Main Strands in Marxism* and D. Anin's *Is Bukharin Topical?* These writings at least permit a discussion with the authors on a sufficiently high professional level which, unfortunately, cannot be said about the obdurate essay by Solzhenitsyn on *Sakharov and the Letter to the Leaders* (no. 2).

However, the worst material in *Kontinent* comes from the pen of its Editor-in-Chief, Vladimir Maximov. And it is not a question of his views or of his attitude, but of his conscious falsification of well-known historical facts. Already in the first editorial of the first copy of *Kontinent*, Maximov wrote that 'in the dark epoch of reactionary Tsarism there came into being in Russia, and there developed *without hindrance*, one of the greatest literatures of mankind. In these times of "slavery" nobody . . . had to look for a publisher abroad. All authors of some prominence, we are underlining *all*, were published in their country.' (*Kontinent*, no. 1, p. 3). But all this is obviously misinforming the Western reader. Wasn't Radishchev exiled to Siberia for his *Journey from Petersburg to Moscow*? Wasn't it from his suicide that our XIX century literature began? And the destruction of Rileyev, the exile of Kukhelbekker, the deportation of Shevchenko, of Chernyshevsky, the forced labour of Dostoyevsky, were they not the result of 'political considerations'? And was Griboyedov's *'Tis Folly to be Wise* published during the lifetime of its author? Wasn't one third of Pushkin's poems secretly circulated in manuscript till the author's death? Can one explain the suicidal death of Pushkin and Lermontov in duels by private reasons only? And the emigration of Herzen and Ogarev, and the whole epos of the *Polar Star* and *The Bell*? And the death of Polezhaev? Not long ago the libraries of Moscow and Leningrad made a list of those many hundreds of artistic works by Russian writers which were banned by the censorship in the XIX century and could only appear abroad. Not a few of Tolstoy's writings circulated secretly in manuscript and first saw the light of day in Europe.

In No. 2 of *Kontinent*, in the 'Editor's Column', Maximov writes, addressing himself to Left-wing groups in the West: 'Certain circles—with a flourish worthy of a better cause—have recently provoked a hysteria about repressions in Chile (two thousand prisoners!) . . . What would these zealots of freedom and humanitarianism say, for whom and in the name of what will they stir up the whole world now, when all, we repeat all, political prisoners in Chile have already been released.' (No. 2, pp. 468-469) The clamour and insistence with which Maximov repeats this well-known lie is indeed worthy of a better cause. Of course, the defence of Soviet writers and Soviet dissenters against political repression (it is with this that Maximov begins his Editor's Column) is an important and noble action. But why should one at the same time minimize or even justify inhuman repressions in Chile and in some other countries of Western Europe? Such deliberate bad faith can in no way benefit *Kontinent*; it will only repel prospective contributors-oppositionists from both inside the USSR and outside it. This makes me think that with an editor like Maximov the failure of the journal is unavoidable.

Against the new messianism

Of course, the experience of Russia and the USSR is very great and other countries must take account of it. In addition that experience was gained at too high a price. But it is in no way Universal, and we are the ones who must make it primarily our own, here in our own country. And if it is right to reject the view that the solution of Soviet problems can come from outside as a result of foreign pressure, then it is even more necessary to give a decisive rejection to the attempt to revive a new form of Russian messianism: that is the view put out by some groups of Russian dissidents who say that only Russia because of all its suffering in the twentieth century can show the world the true way. On the jacket of the first issue of *Kontinent* there appear Solzhenitsyn's words that 'the intellectuals of Eastern Europe speak with the combined voice of suffering and knowledge' and that Western Europe will soon meet its own sorrow 'if its ear remains indifferent'. But has not Western Europe in the twentieth century gone through the terrible experiences of two world wars, several revolutions, the fascist 'New Order' with its totalitarianism, its genocide and its gas chambers, and the experience of several bloody colonial wars? Why cannot Europe find the solution to its own problems, without repeating Russia's mistakes?

How much of this self-confident messianism appears in Shafarevich's articles? 'Russia's way of resurrection is the one on which mankind can find the way out of the impasse, find salvation from the mad race of industrial society, the cult of power, and the gloom of unbelief. We are *the first* to have reached the point where *the uniqueness* of this way can be seen. It is up to *us* to set off along it and *show it to others* . . . The past half century has enriched *us* with an experience *which no other country in the world has had* . . . Russia's position is this: it has gone through death and can hear the voice of God' (*From Under the Heap of Rubbish*, pages 275-6. My underlining—RM). These attempts by Shafarevich, Maximov, and Solzhenitsyn to set themselves up as mankind's teachers seem bound to fail.

One should not ignore the real situation

How do Shafarevich, Solzhenitsyn and their sympathizers propose to solve our difficult problems and cure society's social ills?

'The way to freedom', Shafarevich writes, 'begins inside ourselves, by stopping the climb up the ladder of careerism and the search for material well-being' (*From Under the Heap of Rubbish*, page 269). Any Marxist revolutionary can agree with this. The question is *why* should a person give up his material well-being. Shafarevich believes you should do this not for the sake of art or literature or scientific knowledge because even without all the millions of experts and expensive laboratories it is possible to get to know 'the divine beauty of nature' and the 'divine design'. Solzhenitsyn and Shafarevich maintain that society's social ills can only be healed by religion, that only Orthodoxy can lead the way to freedom, and that only thanks to the Church should one make sacrifices. 'One must not forget', Shafarevich writes, 'that sphere of culture which can be more important than all others for a nation's healthy existence—religion . . . Probably here is the key to the question: Russia's life, death, or resurrection depends on the efforts made in this field. This is our people's most important field of activity and it demands hundreds of thousands of heads and hands. Let us remember that before the Revolution Russia had 300,000 priests. And of course the only people who can work on this today are those that have renounced the system of values which life offers them now' (*From Under the Heap of Rubbish*, pages 271-2).

Remembering that the collection *Landmarks*, whose spiritual descendants the authors of *From Under the Heap of Rubbish* call themselves, was repudiated by the entire Russian intelligentsia from the Cadets to the Bolsheviks, Solzhenitsyn does not expect the present generation of the Russian intelligentsia to be more condescending towards *From Under the Heap of Rubbish*. So in advance he calls our entire intelligentsia despicable, stupid, cowardly, soulless and sunk in the worries of the petty bourgeoisie. It is not an intelligentsia but only 'a superficially educated group'. The 'central' version of this group is how he describes the Moscow intelligentsia for whom Solzhenitsyn has a special hostility. In spite of its great material privileges and high level of information it continues to cringe before the authorities, he says. Solzhenitsyn sees no hope for a resurrection of Russia in this intelligentsia, but only in a few small groups of religious young people, round which the shape of new structures may begin to form as though round tiny crystals. All these views are nothing but Utopian.

Of course, our intelligentsia has many faults, but also many achievements to its credit which the intelligentsia at the turn of the century did not and could not have. It consists of not only the leading section of our society but a rapidly growing and influential one. Without its active participation no serious changes in Soviet society are possible. But in order to arouse it to action, you have to start from its real position, its real interests and its present view of things.

Expressing his hope for miraculous changes in social awareness, Shafarevich recalls 'the unknown monk Luther' who 'took up the fight against the mightiest power in the world of that time, and apparently went against all social and historic laws'. (*From Under the Heap of Rubbish*, page 263.)

But no. Luther did not act against all social and historic laws. His fight four hundred years ago was not against the church and religion, but for reforms within the existing Christian church, for a renewal of its rotten structures and against the disgraceful practice of selling indulgences. Already the vast majority of German society of that time was ready to accept Luther's ideas, and precisely because of this Luther's popularity and influence grew unexpectedly rapidly even within the aristocracy. But Russia at the end of the 20th century is not Germany in the 16th century and our people remain for the most part indifferent to the religious preaching of Shafarevich and Solzhenitsyn, just as the burghers, peasants and princes of 16th century Germany were indifferent or even hostile to the preaching of the atheists. The only chance of success with our intelligentsia or the working class lies with preaching that is based on the demand for reform, and not on the rejection of socialist society. No-one can turn Russia or Europe back to the 16th century.

April 1975

Contributors to this Book

Roy Medvedev was born in Tiflis in 1925. He and his twin brother Zhores have come to be recognized as the main spokesmen of the socialist opposition within the USSR in recent years. Roy Medvedev's best known *Samizdat* (self-published, or underground) work has been translated into English under the title *Let History Judge* (Macmillan 1972). This is a comprehensive history of Stalinism in the Soviet Union, carefully scrutinizing most of the sources which had previously been available to foreign scholars, but also containing much information which was quite new in the West at the time of its publication.

After his brother had published in the United States a critical account of the rise and fall of Lysenko, Zhores became the victim of various official reprisals, culminating in his compulsory incarceration in a mental hospital in Kaluga in mid-1970. Roy's campaign on behalf of his twin, which attracted support from a very wide range of public figures both in the USSR and outside it, finally secured Zhores' release. An account of this episode was subsequently published as a joint work by both the brothers. It appeared under the title *A Question of Madness* (Macmillan 1971). Zhores was then allowed to leave Russia and took up research work in London. Soon afterwards, he was arbitrarily deprived of his Soviet citizenship, although there was neither any public enquiry nor any specific allegation laid against him.

Roy Medvedev remained in Moscow, from where he published his classic work on socialist democracy, a translation of which was due to appear in England in the autumn of 1975. At the beginning of that year, Roy commenced publishing a new journal in *Samizdat* called *20th Century*. Arrangements are being made for this also to be published in an English language version, by the Merlin Press.

KEN COATES. Former coal-miner and then secretary of the Labour Party's national student movement, now teaches sociology at Nottingham University's Adult Education Department. He is a Director of the Bertrand Russell Peace Foundation and was a founder-member of the Institute for Workers' Control. Author of numerous books and pamphlets on industrial democracy, poverty, and socialist strategy.

YVAN CRAIPEAU. One-time secretary to Leon Trotsky, Yvan Craipeau led the French Trotskyists in the Resistance, and remained secretary of their organization until 1947. Subsequently became an initiator of the New Left movement in France, and has, since 1960, been a member of the executive committee of the Unified Socialist Party (PSU). Author of *Le Mouvement Trotskyste en France*, Syros, 1972.

TAMARA DEUTSCHER. Born in Poland, she was in France when the war broke out, and escaped from the German occupiers disguised as an airman. Since 1940 she has lived in England, where she helped her husband, Isaac Deutscher, with his work on the biographies of Stalin and Trotsky. Since 1967 she has edited several posthumous editions of his writings, and has contributed numerous articles to the learned press. She edited *Not by Politics Alone*, a collection of writings on Lenin, published by Allen & Unwin in 1973.

ERNEST MANDEL, distinguished Belgian Marxist economist, was born in 1923. A member of the war-time Resistance, he was captured three times by the Nazis, escaped twice and was eventually condemned to hard labour and deported to Germany. Became editor of *La Gauche* and member of the economic commission of the Belgian TUC. A prominent leader of the Fourth International, he is author of *Marxist Economic Theory* (Merlin Press, 1968) which has appeared in many languages, and of *Europe vs America?* and *The Formation of the Economic Thought of Karl Marx*, both published by New Left Books.

FRANZ MAREK, eminent Austrian Marxist, former member of the politbureau of the Austrian Communist Party, and editor of its theoretical review, *Weg und Ziel*. Expelled in 1970 with Ernst

Fischer and others, because of his strenuous opposition to the Soviet invasion of Czechoslovakia. Founded the *Wiener Tagebuch* which quickly became a leading journal of the independent left. Author of *The Philosophy of World Revolution*, and co-editor with Ernst Fischer of *Marx in His Own Words* and other works.

MIHAILO MARKOVIĆ, until recently Professor of Philosophy at the University of Belgrade, was dismissed by Government decision when his faculty was suppressed. A former partisan and lifelong communist activist, Markovic has received widespread support during this victimization. Co-founder of the international review *Praxis*, also suppressed in early 1975. Has also been associated with the International Humanist and Ethical Union, and is widely travelled as a lecturer. Two of his many books have appeared in English: *The Contemporary Marx* (Spokesman Books, 1974) and *From Affluence to Praxis* (Ann Arbor, 1974).

RALPH MILIBAND. Professor of Politics at Leeds University, played a distinguished role in the development of socialist thought in England during the rise of the New Left after 1956. An active participant in *New Left Review* from its foundation, he co-founded (with John Saville) *The Socialist Register*, which has appeared annually since 1964. Author of *Parliamentary Socialism* (Merlin Press, first published 1961) and *The State in Capitalist Society* (Weidenfeld & Nicolson, 1969).

GEORGE NOVACK, a leading American Marxist scholar who has been involved in work for civil liberties ever since the Scottsboro' Case in 1932, and was an initiator of the Dewey Commission which enquired into the case of Leon Trotsky and the Moscow Trials. A collaborator of C. Wright Mills (*The Marxists*) and Isaac Deutscher (*The Age of Permanent Revolution*), Novack has published a large number of books on socialist theory and practice, including, most recently, *Humanism & Socialism* (Merit, NY, 1973) and *Democracy and Revolution* (Merit, NY, 1971).

MICHEL PABLO. Former secretary of the Fourth International, imprisoned in Holland for his work in defence of the Algerian Revolution, Michel Pablo (or Raptis, as he is sometimes known) was economic advisor to the Algerian Government of Ben Bella. Between 1972 to 73 he was in Chile at the invitation of the Allende Government, and his analysis of Chilean events was published in 1974 under the title of *Revolution & Counter-Revolution in Chile* (Allison and Busby, London).

ROGER PANNEQUIN. Former member of the Central Committee of the French Communist Party. Led the war-time communist underground in Northern France, and was captured and deported. Is currently an active member of the 'Comité du 5 Janvier' for Czechoslovak freedom and independence.

JIRI PELIKAN. A moving spirit of the Prague Spring of 1968, Jiri Pelikan was head of Czechoslovak television at the time of the Soviet and allied invasion. In exile, he established the periodical *Listy*, which continues to act as a voice of the socialist opposition at home and in emigration. His book *Ici Prague* is about to be translated into English.

E. P. THOMPSON. Co-founder of the *New Reasoner* in England in 1956, which subsequently merged to form *New Left Review*, Edward Thompson was a pioneer of the New Left which arose after the double crisis in Hungary and at Suez. A distinguished historian, he is best known for *The Making of the English Working Class*, which has become an indispensable work for all involved in the field of Labour history.